Have you
I still got
you headache

A SURVEY OF OLD TESTAMENT TEACHING

By

J. WASH WATTS

Volume II

SOLOMON—MALACHI

BROADMAN PRESS
NASHVILLE, TENNESSEE

Printed in United States of America

1.5S622

TO
FELLOW STUDENTS OF THE WORD
WHO DESIRE
TO UNDERSTAND THE BIBLE
IN ORDER THAT
THEY MAY PREACH ITS GOSPEL

A SURVEY OF OLD TESTAMENT TEACHING

Jehovah our God is one Jehovah: and thou shalt love Jehovah thy God with all thy heart, and with all thy soul, and with all thy might. And these words, . . . shall be upon thy heart; *and thou shalt teach them diligently.*

—*Deuteronomy* 6:4-7.

Then opened he [Jesus] their mind that they might understand the scriptures; and he said unto them, . . . *Ye are witnesses of these things.*

—*Luke* 24:45-48.

PREFACE

The *purpose* of this survey is to guide students of the Bible to those viewpoints from which they may continue Old Testament interpretation independently. It will not undertake to do more than lay foundations. It is prepared primarily for use in the author's classes at the New Orleans Baptist Theological Seminary.

While interpreting the Old Testament we interpret also the New Testament. The harmonious linking of the two is the true objective for such a study. We must needs remember that "Jehovah our God is one Jehovah."[1] The example of Jesus in preparing the apostles for the preaching of the gospel is likewise significant, for the Scriptures he used when "he opened their minds that they might understand the scriptures"[2] were Old Testament Scriptures. When he said, "Ye are witnesses of these things,"[3] he referred to truths first taught in the Old Testament.

The *methods* of this study are expected to be historical, exegetical, and theological.

The historical background of authors, books, and language will be sought. Lessons from the history of nations whose influence has a bearing on Israelitic history will be introduced, but this must be done largely through citation of parallel reading. It is understood that archeological and critical reviews of such history are closely dovetailed with interpretation, but the mass of such material requires the handling of it by theological seminaries in a separate department of study. Only brief directions for read-

[1]Deut. 6:4.
[2]Luke 24:45.
[3]Luke 24:48.

ing will be introduced at points where the information is most pertinent. These will direct attention to outstanding matters and investigation to features of vital concern to our conclusions in interpretation.

Exegetical treatments will include outlines of books and textual notes. Outlines present the teaching in a summary fashion. Notes present explanations concerning details of importance, information not available to all, and emphases upon matters of extraordinary concern to us. Outlines are intended to present the prominent points of the writers of the Scriptures rather than points of chief interest to us, and to do so as far as possible according to a logical arrangement that will enable us to observe the consistent development of their teaching. It does matter a great deal to us and to our preaching of the gospel whether or not we think the Old Testament to be consistent and intelligible. Of course no intimation is intended that its men and affairs are always consistent. The question is, Is its message of hope to sinful men, its teaching about "Jehovah," consistent and intelligible?

Theological treatment will attempt to lay foundations of Biblical Theology. Whereas Systematic Theology organizes our beliefs according to a system of its own, Biblical Theology does so with reference to their origin in Scripture, thus according to the order of their development in Scripture. Biblical Theology, therefore, maintains a close contact with biblical history and makes the creeds drawn therefrom clear and interesting. It is obviously impossible to give in our work a full treatment of this theology; but, while attention is centered on the history, attempts will be made to lay foundations.

In any theological treatment, the principles of development are of course the conceptions of authors about God. As the Old Testament authors build their teaching concerning God chiefly about the name "Jehovah," the interpretation of "Jehovah" worship must be a paramount issue. From the time when this name first appears on the lips of Eve at the birth of her first-born son, through the great revelations to Moses that make this name a synonym for the moral attributes of God, and in all the teaching of all the prophets, we are led step by step to the conviction that the "Jehovah" of the Old Testament is identified with the Jesus of the New Testament. Accordingly, the fulfilment of all is predicted by the following word of Zechariah as coming in Messiah, "And Jehovah shall be king over all the earth: in that day shall Jehovah be one, and his name one."[4] No amount of care is too dear a price for any student of the Scriptures to pay in order to attain an unclouded view of this truth. We must needs consider this the main objective of all our work.

In all these methods scientific correctness is necessary, but scientific methods need not exclude the phenomena of revelation and faith as credible data. Revelation and faith are naturally not subjects for consideration in a science which deals with material matter only, but they are vital to a science

[4] Zech. 14:9.

that is supremely spiritual. In the words of James Orr, "It is Christ Himself in the full revelation of His glory as the only-begotten Son who is the touch-stone and measure of the supernatural for faith; and only that view of revelation in Israel is adequate which finds its necessary culmination in His person and redemption."[5]

We admit that *our starting viewpoint is one of faith in the trustworthiness of the Bible.* We desire to submit our convictions to objective investigation according to the strictest standards of criticism. Nevertheless, we also believe that it is as scientifically correct for the believer to start from the viewpoint of faith as it is for scientists to start from the viewpoint of any current hypothesis of material science with a view to testing it. Moreover, we believe that the results depend largely upon choice of the right hypothesis. As a surveyor, having found certain old landmarks recorded on a plat of land, runs a line according to them with a view to locating others described by that same plat; so may a believer, who has found in Christ a Saviour and in many prophetical Scriptures landmarks leading to him, reasonably run a line by faith backward in search of earlier revelations belonging to the same plan indicated by his Bible. The finding of these revelations is likely to depend upon the zeal and judgment with which the believer tests his own convictions about the Bible. The problem is intricate, the issue vital to spiritual development, and the cost fully worth while.

[5]Orr, James, *Problems of the Old Testament*, p. 22.

The class use of these outlines will include direct Bible study under their guidance, parallel investigation, and class discussion.

The textbooks are the American Standard Edition of the Bible and this volume. The biblical text serves as the basis for all work, and this volume as a syllabus.

Quotations from Scripture, unless otherwise noted, are from the American Standard Version.

The inspiration and advice of many teachers and friends have contributed to this work in ways too numerous to mention. Two co-workers have rendered valuable aid in the preparation of copy: Rev. J. Hardee Kennedy and Rev. Jesse L. Boyd, Jr.

J. WASH WATTS

New Orleans, Louisiana

CONTENTS

OBADIAH

JOEL

JONAH

AMOS

HOSEA

ABBREVIATIONS FOR WORKS FREQUENTLY USED

MT—Massoretic Text of the Hebrew Old Testament

MTG—Massoretic Text compiled by C. D. Ginsburg

MTK—Massoretic Text arranged by Rud. Kittel in *Biblia Hebraica*

LXX—*The Septuagint,* first translation of the Old Testament, in Greek, made by Jews in Egypt about 275-150 B.C.

Vul—*The Vulgate,* official translation of the Roman Catholic Church, in Latin, made by Jerome about A.D. 390-405

DV—*Douay Version,* English translation of the Vulgate, made in England in A.D. 1609

AV—*Authorized Version,* English translation authorized by King James I of England in A.D. 1611

ERV—*English Revised Version,* made in England by a group of scholars gathered from all Protestant denominations, published in A.D. 1885

ASV—*American Standard Version,* made in America by a group of scholars from all Protestant denominations, published in A.D. 1901

MNT—*A New Translation* by James Moffatt, published in 1922

AT—*An American Translation* by J. M. Powis Smith and a group of scholars, published in 1927

SBD—*Smith's Bible Dictionary*

HDB—*Hasting's Dictionary of the Bible*

ISBE—*International Standard Bible Encyclopaedia*

LOT—*Introduction to the Literature of the Old Testament,* by S. R. Driver

POT—*The Problem of the Old Testament,* by James Orr

MOT—*The Monuments and the Old Testament,* by Ira M. Price

BB—*Biblical Backgrounds,* by J. McKee Adams

HTE—*His Truth Endureth,* by James C. Muir

OTTO—*Old Testament Theology,* by Gustav F. Oehler

OTTS—*Old Testament Theology,* by Herman Schultz

TOT—*Theology of the Old Testament,* by A. B. Davidson

TS—*Typology of Scripture,* by Patrick Fairbairn

CB—*Cambridge Bible for Schools and Colleges*

CC—*Calvin's Commentary*

EB—*The Expositor's Bible*

ICC—*International Critical Commentary*

CPC—*Clarke's People's Commentary*

AC—*The American Commentary*

BC—*The Bible Commentary*

PC—*The Pulpit Commentary*

HC—*The Homiletical Commentary*

CWB—*A Commentary on the Whole Bible,* by Matthew Henry

IEB—*An Interpretation of the English Bible,* by B. H. Carroll

CHS—*A Commentary on the Holy Scriptures,* by Peter Lange

PB—*The People's Commentary,* by Joseph Parker

EHS—*Expositions of Holy Scriptures,* by Alexander Maclaren

INTRODUCTION TO KINGS
AND II CHRONICLES

Parallel Reading

Stearns, W. N., "Books of Kings," in *ISBE*.

Burney, C. F., "Kings I and II," in *HDB*.

Driver, S. R., "I and II Kings," in *LOT*, pp. 175-193.

Beecher, W. J., "Books of Chronicles," in *ISBE*.

Brown, Francis, "Chronicles I and II," in *HDB*.

Driver, S. R., "Chronicles," in *LOT*, pp. 484-506.

Names

The Hebrew title for the books of Kings is simply "Kings." Division into "The First Book of Kings" and "The Second Book of Kings" follows the LXX. The LXX likewise gave us two books of Samuel. Putting these four under the title, "Books of Kingdoms," the LXX listed the books of Samuel as first and second, the books of Kings as third and fourth. Its treatment emphasizes the close connection between Samuel and Kings, and also the fact that both deal with the kingdom, but it leads to an unnatural division within each of them. The Hebrew Canon treats each as a single book, and many facts concerning contents make it seem well for us to follow its usage.

The name "Chronicles," literally, "The Words (or Affairs) of the Days," is the equivalent of journal. Since it refers, in the case of 2 Chronicles, chiefly to the kings of Judah, the parallel to Kings is obvious. Second Chronicles is often reckoned with 1 Chronicles as one book. However, both ways of counting are said to have been used as far back as

[1]

our knowledge goes.[1] In this case, the division into
two books is more natural than in Kings because
1 Chronicles parallels Samuel while 2 Chronicles
parallels Kings.

Dates and Authors

Concerning the authors who put together these
books as we now have them, we have no definite information.

As to dates, the closing passages in both cases
furnish evidence as to the earliest possible dates.
As 2 Kings 25:27 mentions the thirty-seventh year
of Judah's captivity, we look upon the period of the
Captivity as the most probable time for the final
work on Kings. As 2 Chronicles 36:22-23 speaks of
the edict of Cyrus concerning the return, we must
look to the period following the return for the final
work on 2 Chronicles. There is much dispute as to
definite suggestions, but connections between 2
Chronicles and Ezra-Nehemiah make the period of
Nehemiah most likely.

Purposes

The purpose of Kings is to tell of the taking away
of the kingdom. This is revealed by a series of emphases upon prophecies concerning the taking away
of the kingdom and their fulfilment. As Samuel tells
of the establishment of the kingdom, so Kings tells
how it is torn asunder and its people carried into
captivity. Samuel traces the development from the
unorganized state existing in the days of the judges
to the unity attained under David. Kings traces the

---

[1]Beecher, Willis J., "Books of Chronicles," ISBE, p. 630.

breaking up of that unity from its beginning in the reign of Solomon to its completion in the Exile.

The purpose of 2 Chronicles apparently is to supplement the records concerning the kings of Judah. It mentions the kings of Israel only as they affect the kings of Judah. Like 1 Chronicles, it adds much information concerning the Davidic line not given in other narratives. This fact is emphasized in the name given these books in the LXX, *Paraleipomenon*, "Of Things Left Untold."

Methods

The difference in purposes helps us to understand a difference in methods, which is of great importance to our study. Second Chronicles is a loosely joined collection of narratives with occasional interpretations but without a great unifying message. All parts of Kings are closely tied and effectively arranged by a prophetic interpretation of the great turns in the history. This prophetical interpretation uses the facts of history so as to give explanations of history, ethical applications of the will of God to affairs of state, and implications concerning the meaning of prophecy.

This arrangement of the message in Kings offers an explanation for many other facts concerning the structure of the book which have puzzled students of it a great deal.

The division in the account of Rehoboam in 1 Kings is an example of these puzzling facts. One part is given in 12:1-20, the other in 14:21-31. Chapter divisions, topical notes, and commentators' outlines fail to reveal a recognition of the purpose behind this division. From the viewpoint of the observations made above, it appears to be due to the fact that information about Rehoboam is not a chief point in the message at any time. Instead, the rending of the kingdom in the days of Solomon and his son is the first chief topic, and the first account of Rehoboam merely gives evidence of fulfilment of Ahijah's prophecy concerning that rending. Likewise, the taking of the kingdom from the house of Jeroboam I is the second chief topic, and the second account of Rehoboam is merely a link in a chain of evidence showing fulfilment of another prophecy by Ahijah which foretells that taking away of the kingdom.

A similar method of using the history of the kings of Judah is continued in Kings until all messages concerning the Northern Kingdom are fulfilled. Then messages concerning Judah become keys to its arrangement, and this continues to the end.

Chapter divisions throughout the book reveal no recognition of the order of the message. The division into the two books breaks into the middle of the message concerning the taking of the kingdom from the house of Ahab. Commentaries, moreover, have fallen into the habit of dividing the message according to the reigns of individual kings after the fashion of 2 Chronicles. All such treatment helps to obscure the message rather than to clarify it.

Only as we observe closely this arrangement around the prophecies can we fully appreciate the message. Then its use of historical data becomes

clear and effective. Then the prophetic utterances
stand out as milestones marking a way of salvation
that runs from the dawn of time through our own
age unto the end of days. Then the sweeping power
of its terrible warnings can be brought into this
brief, general outline:

I. Rending of the Kingdom in the Days of Solo-·
mon and His Son

II. Taking of the Kingdom from the House of
Jeroboam

III. Taking of the Kingdom from the House of
Baasha

IV. Taking of the Kingdom from the House of
Ahab

V. Taking of the Kingdom from the House of
Jehu

VI. Taking of the Kingdom from All the Seed of
Israel

VII. Taking of the Kingdom from Judah

DETAILED OUTLINE

Taking Away of the Kingdom

I

Rending of the Kingdom in the Days of Solomon
and His Son

1 Kings 1:1 to 12:24. Cf. 2 Chronicles Chaps. 1-12
Key passages: 3:1-15; 9:1-9; 11:9-13, 26-40;
12:21-24

1. Solomon is established as king, according
to directions of David..............1:1 to 2:46

(1) His crowning is provoked by
Adonijah's rebellion 1:1-53

(2) He carries out the advice of
David to remove Adonijah,
Joab, Abiathar, and Shemei 2:1-46

2. He is established over all Israel, according to the Word of JHWH..........3:1 to 10:29

(1) According to a vision at Gibeon
........................3:1 to 8:66
Int. The vision 3:1-15
He is assured of wisdom, riches,
and honor because of his prayer;
and permanent blessing, if obedient.

a. A wise judgment makes the people fear him 3:16-28

b. His organization of the realm,
extension of power, wealth, and
literary labors create a worldwide reputation 4:1-34

c. His building of the Temple and
prayer of dedication bring a
manifestation of the presence of
JHWH ....5:1 to 8:66

(2) According to a second vision 9:1 to 10:29
Int. The vision 9:1-9
He is assured of perpetual care
for the Temple and of permanence for his kingdom, if he is
obedient

a. Prosperity for Solomon on all
sides 9:10-28
b. The visit of the Queen of Sheba
pays tribute to his wisdom..10:1-13
c. Unparalleled amount of tribute
........................10:14-29

3. In the end his kingdom is rent because
of disobedience ....11:1 to 12:24
Int. His love for foreign women......11:1-8
(1) JHWH declares that he will rend
his kingdom in the days of his son
.............................11:9-13
(2) JHWH raises up adversaries..11:14-40
a. Hadad, the Edomite.......11:14-22
b. Rezon of Syria............11:23-25
c. Jeroboam, the son of Nebat.11:26-40
Ahijah, the Shilonite, prophesies
his rule over Israel and promises
a permanent blessing like
David's, if he is obedient.

(3) Israel, the Ten Tribes, revolt at
Shechem ....11:41 to 12:24
Int. Death of Solomon........11:41-43
a. Rehoboam refuses to reduce
taxation 12:1-15
b. The ten tribes make Jeroboam
king 12:16-20
c. Shemaiah leads Judah to accept
the division as the will of JHWH
........................12:21-24

II

Taking of the Kingdom from the House of Jeroboam
1 Kings 12:25-15:32. Cf. 2 Chronicles 13:1 to 14:1

Key passages: 14:13-16; 15:29

1. Jeroboam makes Israel to sin..........12:25-33
   (1) He makes golden calves for Israel's
       gods 12:25-28
   (2) He changes the place of worship
       ....12:29-30
   (3) He changes the priesthood.......12:31
   (4) He changes the time of the feast.12:32a
   (5) He goes up unto the altar....12:32b-33
2. A man of God from Judah predicts dese-
   cration of Jeroboam's altar at Bethel by
   a king of Judah to be named Josiah......13:1-34
3. The house of Jeroboam is cut off according to the prophecy of Ahijah, the Shilonite ....14:1 to 15:32
   (1) The wife of Jeroboam goes to Ahi-
       jah to inquire concerning her sick
       child and is told that he will die up-
       on her return, all others will die
       violently, and Israel will finally go
       into captivity because of the sins
       of Jeroboam 14:1-16
   (2) The prophecy concerning the sick
       child is fulfilled immediately..14:17-18
   (3) Historical records show the cutting
       off of the line in the days of Nadab
       ....14:19 to 15:32

III

Taking of the Kingdom from the House of Baasha
1 Kings 15:33 to 16:14. Cf. 2 Chronicles 14:2 to
16:10
Key passages: 16:1-4, 12

1. Baasha walks in the sins of Jeroboam . . 15:33-34
2. Jehu, the son of Hanani, prophesies that
   JHWH will utterly sweep away the
   house of Baasha 16:1-7
3. Elah and all the house of Baasha slain
   by Zimri 16-8-14

IV

Taking of the Kingdom from the House of Ahab
1 Kings 16:15-2 Kings 10:17. Cf. 2 Chronicles
16:11-22:9
Key passages: 16:29-34; 19:16; 20:42; 21:17-29;
22:37-38; 1:17-18; 9:24-26, 36; 10:11, 17

Int. Historical records which show its es-
tablishment 16:15-28
The house which is later called by the
prophets the House of Ahab was started
by Omri, who slew Zimri after he had
reigned only seven days.

1. Ahab does more evil than his predeces-
   sors 16:29-34
   (1) He walks in the sins of Jeroboam
   . . . . 16:29-30
   (2) He marries Jezebel of Sidon 16:31
   (3) The abominations of Baal worship
   are introduced 16:32-34

2. Elijah is led to select a successor for
   Ahab ....17:1 to 19:21
   (1) He proclaims a drought for three
       and one-half years............17:1-24
   (2) He destroys four hundred and fifty
       prophets of Baal at Mount Carmel,
       then prays for rain 18:1-46
   (3) Because Ahab still listens to Jezebel,
       he flees to Mount Sinai and is in-
       structed by JHWH to anoint the
       following: Hazael to be king over
       Syria, Jehu to be king over Israel,
       and Elisha to be prophet in his stead
       ....19:1-21
3. An unnamed prophet prophesies the
   death of Ahab 20:1-43
   (1) Ahab wins a victory over the
       Syrians according to a prophet's
       instructions 20:1-21
   (2) JHWH delivers the Syrians, in-
       cluding king Ben-hadad, into the
       hands of Ahab that Ahab might
       recognize JHWH, but he releases
       Ben-hadad for the sake of a trade
       agreement 20:22-34
   (3) Another prophet dramatically pro-
       claims that Ahab's life will be re-
       quired in the place of Ben-hadad's
       ....20:35-43
4. Elijah prophesies that the house of
   Ahab will be cut off 21:1-29

(3) He dies as predicted and another
son of Ahab, Jehoram, succeeds him
...........................1:17-18

7. Elisha brings about the end........2:1 to 10:17
   Int. The mantle of Elijah falls on
   Elisha 2:1-25

(1) Elisha pursues a helpful ministry
through many years ....3:1 to 8:6
   a. He predicts victory over Moab 3:1-27
   b. He works miracles to relieve the
      people ....4:1 to 7:20
      (a) A widow from debt ...4:1-7
      (b) The Shunammite from
          sorrow 4:8-37
      (c) The prophets from
          hunger 4:38-44
      (d) Naaman, the Syrian,
          from leprosy 5:1-27
      (e) The prophets from lack
          of shelter 6:1-7
      (f) The whole land from
          raiding bands of Syrians
          ....6:8-23
      (g) Samaria from starva-
          tion ....6:24 to 7:20
   c. Testimony concerning "all the
      great things" that Elisha did
      ....8:1-6

(2) Hazael becomes king of Syria according to the prophecy of Elisha 8:7-15

V

Taking of the Kingdom from the House of Jehu

2 Kings 10:18 to 15:12. Cf. 2 Chronicles 22:10 to 26:23 and Amos

Key passages: 10:30-31; 15:12

1. Jehu destroys Baal out of Israel but does not depart from the sins of Jeroboam..10:18-29
2. JHWH promises Jehu that his sons unto the fourth generation will reign over Israel, but Jehu remains disobedient....10:30-31
3. JHWH begins even in Jehu's day to cut off from Israel by the hand of Hazael..10:32-36 (The line of David is preserved by the rescue of Joash from Athaliah's slaughter of the royal seed ....11:1 to 12:21)

4. Jehoahaz continues in the sins of Jeroboam, and JHWH continues to deliver Israel into the hands of Hazael..........13:1-9
5. Jehoash defeats Ben-hadad of Syria three times, as prophesied by Elisha, conquers Amaziah of Judah, but also continues in the sins of Jeroboam.13:10 to 14:16
6. Jeroboam II greatly extends the borders of Israel, as prophesied by Jonah, but does not depart from the sins of Jeroboam I 14:17-29
7. Zechariah, a son of the fourth generation from Jehu, is slain by Shallum..........15:1-12

VI

Taking of the Kingdom from All the Seed of Israel

2 Kings 15:13 to 17:41. Cf. 2 Chronicles 27:1 to 31:21, Amos and Hosea

Key passage: 17:7-41 (especially v. 20)

1. Shallum is slain by Menahem after one month 15:13-16
2. Menahem pays tribute to Pul of Assyria to have the kingdom confirmed in his hands 15:17-22
3. Pekahiah, the son of Menahem, is slain by Pekah after two years 15:23-26
4. Parts of Israel are carried captive to Assyria, and Pekah is slain by Hoshea ....15:27 to 16:20
5. Hoshea conspires with Egypt against Assyria and is carried into captivity with the remainder of the people by Sargon ..17:1-41

VII

Taking of the Kingdom from Judah

2 Kings 18:1 to 25:30. Cf. 2 Chronicles 32:1 to
36:23, Isaiah, chapters 1-39, Micah, Habakkuk,
Zephaniah, Jeremiah, Ezekiel

Key passages: 19:14-21, 33-37; 20:16-18; 21:10-15;
22:16-20, 23:26-27; 24:3-4, 20; 25:21

1. According to the word of Isaiah....18:1 to 20:21
   (1) Because of Hezekiah's prayer, the
       nation is spared during Sennache-
       rib's invasion ....18:1 to 19:37
   (2) Yet, when Hezekiah shows the
       treasures of Jerusalem to the mes-
       sengers of Berodach-baladan, cap-
       tivity in Babylon is prophesied 20:1-21
2. Because of the abominations of Manasseh, the casting off by JHWH of the remnant of his inheritance is announced by
   his servants the prophets 21:1-18
3. According to the word of Huldah, the
   prophetess, after the discovery of the
   book of the law in the Temple, every
   remnant is removed ....21:19 to 25:30
   Int. Because of Josiah's fear of JHWH
       and his great reforms, the nation is
       spared in his day ......21:19 to 23:25
   (1) Josiah dies from wounds received
       in battle with Pharaoh-necho 23:26-30
   (2) Jehoahaz is carried into Egypt by
       Pharaoh-necho and dies there..23:31-35

(3) Bands of Chaldeans, Syrians, and Moabites are sent against Judah in the days of Jehoiakim....23:36 to 24:7

(4) Jehoiachin, with ten thousand other captives and the treasures of Jerusalem, including those of the house of JHWH, are carried to Babylon by Nebuchadnezzar 24:8-17

(5) Zedekiah, the last king of Judah, is carried captive to Babylon, his sons slain, and his eyes put out 24:18 to 25:7

(6) The residue of the people, except the poorest, are likewise carried away 25:8-21

(7) Gedaliah, the governor of the miserable remnant left in the land, is slain; and all others left in the land go down into Egypt..........25:22-30

Chronological Chart for Study of Kings and II Chronicles

Approximate Dates	Kings of Judah (House of David)	Approximate Dates	Kings of Israel (Ten Tribes)	Prophets and Contemporary Events
972 B.C.		Solomon over all Israel		Nathan
40 years				Shishak overthrows Tanite Dynasty in Egypt
933	1. Rehoboam	933 — 22 yrs.	1. Jeroboam (House of: Jeroboam)	Ahijah the Shilonite
17	2. Abijah	2	2. Nadab	Shemaiah in Judah
				An unnamed prophet in Israel
3	3. Asa	24	3. Baasha (House of: Baasha)	Iddo in Judah
				Zerah of Ethiopia defeated by Asa
				Azariah in Judah
		2	4. Elah	Benhadad I of Syria hired by Asa to attack Israel
		(7 days)	5. Zimri	Hanani in Judah
		12	6. Omri	Jehu, the son of Hanani in Israel
				Benhadad II reigns in Syria
41	4. Jehoshaphat	22	7. Ahab (House of:— Ahab)	Shalmaneser III reigns in Assyria
				Elijah in Israel
				Unnamed prophets in Israel
				Jehu in Judah
				Micaiah in Israel
				400 false prophets in Israel
				Jahaziel in Judah
25	5. Jehoram	2	8. Ahaziah	Eliezer in Judah
				Elisha in Israel
8	6. Ahaziah (Athaliah)	12	9. Jehoram	Obadiah (?) in Judah
				Mesha reigns in Moab
1		843 — 12	10. Jehu (Jehu)	Hadadeser (Benhadad II) in Syria slain and succeeded by Hazael.
843				

NOTE: Athaliah is not numbered, because she was a usurper, not of the line of David.

Chronological Chart for Study of Kings and II Chronicles (Con'd)

Approximate Dates	Kings of Judah (House of David)	Approximate Dates	Kings of Israel (Ten Tribes) (House of Jehu)	Prophets and Contemporary Events
843 B.C.	(Athaliah)	843 B.C.	10. Jehu	Shalmaneser III attacks Hazael
6	7. Joash	28	11. Jehoahaz	Joel (?) in Judah
40	8. Amaziah	17	12. Jehoash	Zechariah, son of Jehoida, in Judah
		16	13. Jeroboam II	Hazael threatens Jerusalem
29	9. Uzziah	41		Benhadad III in Syria
				An unnamed prophet in Judah
				Another unnamed prophet in Judah
				Jonah in Israel
		(6 mo.)	14. Zechariah	Zechariah in Judah
52	10. Jotham	(1 mo.)	15. Shallum	Amos of Judah in Israel
		10	16. Menahem	Hosea in Israel
		2	17. Pekahiah	Tiglath-pileser III (Pul) reigns in Assyria (745-727)
16	11. Ahaz	20	18. Pekah	Isaiah in Judah
				Rezin reigns in Syria
				Micah in Judah
16	12. Hezekiah	9	19. Hoshea	Damascus taken by Pul of Assyria
				Oded in Israel
		721	(Destruction of Samaria)	Shalmaneser V reigns in Assyria
721				Sargon II reigns in Assyria

Chronological Chart for Study of Kings and II Chronicles (Con'd)

Approximate Dates	Kings of Judah	Prophets	Contemporary Events in Assyria, Babylonia, and Egypt
721 B.C.	Hezekiah (Con'd)	Isaiah (Con'd)	Sargon's reign in Assyria (Con'd)
		Micah (Con'd)	Merodach-baladan of Babylon overthrown by Sargon
			Sennacherib of Assyria invades Judah (701)
			Tirhakah of Egypt makes war with Sennacherib
29	13. Manasseh		Esarhaddon reigns in Assyria
55			Esarhaddon of Assyria conquers Egypt
2	14. Amon	Nahum in Judah	Assurbanipal reigns in Babylon
31	15. Josiah	Jeremiah in Judah	Egypt again invaded by Assyrians and Thebes sacked
		Zephaniah in Judah	
609	16. Jehoahaz	Huldah the prophetess in Judah	Nabo-polassar reigns in Babylon
(3 mo.)		Habakkuk in Judah	Nineveh destroyed
608	17. Jehoiakim (Beginning of captivity)	Daniel in the city of Babylon	Pharaoh-necho of Egypt is defeated by Nebuchadnezzar at Carchemish (605)
605			
11		Ezekiel among Jewish exiles in Babylon	Nebuchadnezzar reigns in Babylon
11			
597	18. Jehoiachin	Jeremiah forced by the last Jewish remnant in the land to go with it into Egypt	Pharaoh-hophra leads Zedekiah to rebel against Nebuchadnezzar.
(3 mo.)			
597	19. Zedekiah		
587	(Destruction of Jerusalem. The people left in Judah go down to Egypt.)		

House of David

TEXTUAL NOTES

Outline of Solomon's Reign

Comments here and there in the text indicate the outline of Solomon's reign as the author of Kings saw it.

In 2:12 one is found which shows that he thought of the events in chapters 1 and 2 as serving to establish Solomon as king.

In 4:1 and 8:66 he observes that Solomon was established over all Israel, not merely in name, but also to the satisfaction of his people.

In 11:1, however, there is a turn. The "now" at the beginning of this verse could be "but," and probably should be. The author begins here a description of dissatisfaction and disruption which spoiled the glory of Solomon's reign.

Thus we see three main periods in Solomon's reign. The first pictures its establishment as David directed, the second its establishment in the favor of all the people, and the third its turn downward unto dissolution. Building on the foundations laid by David, Solomon proceeded to a wonderful height in wisdom, riches, and honor. Nevertheless, elements of spiritual failure and decay which had been develing throughout his reign spoiled his achievement in the end.

Prophetic Interpretation of Solomon's Reign

The keys to the prophetical judgment of Solomon appear in 3:1-15; 9:1-9; and in 11:9-13. The judgment itself is described in 11:26-40 and 12:21-24.

References in 9:2 to the first vision and in 11:9 to
the two visions show how these matters were linked
together in the author's interpretation.

The promises in 3:12-13 concerning wisdom,
riches, and honor are given with assurance of fulfilment. Not so the one concerning length of days!
Emphasis upon the condition, "if thou wilt walk in
my ways," is significant.

The promise concerning wisdom received its first
fulfilment in the wise judgment which proved the
love of a mother for her child. The close connection
is shown by the first words of 3:16, which should be
rendered, "Then proceeded to come." In other
words, the author saw the coming of the women as
an immediate test of Solomon's wisdom.

The promise concerning riches and honor is seen
as fulfilled in the accounts of 4:1-34.

The account of 5:1 to 8:66, leading up to the
dedication of the Temple, the manifestation of
JHWH's presence, and the satisfaction of the people
brings the fulfilment of these promises to a climax.
The story of the Temple building and dedication is
a typical illustration of the fact that Kings never
drops to the level of a bare historical chronicle but is
throughout an interpretation of the history.

The coming of the second vision immediately
after the climax pictured in 8:66 makes the stern
warning in 9:4-9 stand out in bold contrast. The
tentative promise of permanence was given in one
verse in the first vision. In the second, the message is almost entirely devoted to it. Moreover,

after another brief discussion of this condition of fulfilment, "if thou wilt walk before me as David thy father walked," emphasis is laid on the opposite, "if ye shall turn away from following me."

The records in 9:10 to 10:29 show the wisdom, riches, and honor continuing in a great way, so far as outward appearances are concerned. Speculation may discern even here things beneath the surface that were not great and fine, but the show was going on in all its glory when the Queen of Sheba came.

The actual result is prophesied in 11:11-12. The prediction of complete fulfilment in the days of Solomon's son shows that the revolt of the Ten Tribes against Rehoboam is an essential part of this interpretation of Solomon's reign.

Ahijah's rending of his garment and giving of ten pieces to Jeroboam is another link with this conclusion.

Shemaiah's interpretation of the actual revolt as the work of JHWH brings this particular message to a close.

Miscellaneous

4:29-34. This passage is warrant for the opinion that the influence of Solomon was foremost in creation of the "wisdom" literature. His influence will be in question when we come to a study of Proverbs, Ecclesiastes, and the Song of Solomon. Regardless of opinions concerning the authorship, the influence of his literary labors and his reputation for wisdom must be given a prominent place in the developments producing this literature.

8:27. This recognition of the omnipresence of God is very instructive. The occurrence of this expression of conviction immediately after the appearance of the glory of JHWH recorded in 8:10-11 shows that Solomon and his people looked upon the Temple and the cloud of glory as mere symbols of the presence of JHWH. Accordingly, they did not consider him a local deity. This does not say that all the people had this high vision of God, but the faithful did.

8:46. The parenthesis in this verse expresses the belief that all men are sinners as clearly as any point in the Bible. When we add the expectation that repentance and faith in JHWH will secure forgiveness for sin, which is found throughout the dedicatory prayer, we have the fundamentals of the plan of salvation.

9:14. The statement in 9:11 that Hiram had furnished Solomon "according to all his desire" makes a contrast with Solomon's response. Solomon's gift to Hiram was not appreciated, and Hiram called the cities *Cabul,* which is thought to mean "as good as nothing,"[2] Yet Hiram sent six score talents of gold to Solomon. We have no means of comparing the value of the gold to the value of the cities. The tone of this passage, however, seems to represent this transaction as a bit of sharp practice on Solomon's part.

9:15-22. The levy spoken of was a body of conscripted laborers. According to 5:13, this group

[2]Brown, Driver, and Briggs, A Hebrew and English Lexicon of the Old Testament, p. 459.

numbered thirty thousand. 5:15 mentions two other armies of laborers, one of seventy thousand, the other of eighty thousand, which worked in Palestine only. The first, however, was sent by courses to the Lebanon mountains during the work on the Temple. The present description of its work shows that its conscription was first occasioned by Pharaoh's gift of Gezer to his daughter. That start in unwelcome relations with foreigners is pictured as leading to a very extensive building program. A large part of that program was for military purposes. Doubtless there was no objection to the work on the Temple. Much of it, however, constituted the burdens so bitterly complained of by the assembly of Israel when Rehoboam succeeded Solomon.

9:24. The exclamatory "but" points to the use of Solomon's great building program to give foremost honor and luxury to a heathen princess.

10:14-22. The 666 talents of gold, mentioned as Solomon's yearly amount of revenue, is reckoned as about twenty million dollars. Much of it came from foreign sources. Nevertheless, the draft upon his own people for labor leaders, government officials, army, and navy drained their man power so as to make the means of securing this huge amount of tribute a burden. The government was getting rich, but not the people. In time this plan crushed the nation. There is a tremendous lesson in this. Income drawn from the fruits of people's own labor will surely give strength to their organization, but income drawn by oppression from the fruits of other people's labor will eventually weaken their organization.

10:23-29. Solomon's building of an army and traffic in armaments is another part of this oppressive program. The traffic is described in 10:29. Horses had been but little used in the land. They were not brought in for work but as chariot horses. Solomon also bought and sold them for profit. This profit was probably used as one of the excuses for building a big army. It could not, however, keep the militaristic program from becoming oppressive.

Developments of these matters appear as follows: (1) riches are gathered largely by the despoiling of others; (2) a large army is built to protect the riches; (3) expenditure according to the pleasure of the monarch (Cf. 9:19), ostentatious splendor (Cf. 10:16-22), and moral decay (Cf. 11:1-8) grow under the protection of this militaristic policy.

11:1-8. Marriage with "many foreign women" was doubtless another result of policies intended to promote the welfare of Solomon's government. Many of his marriages, as in the case of Pharaoh's daughter, did secure alliances with surrounding nations, which at first promoted peace, trade, and prosperity. Nevertheless, they were undertaken contrary to the will of JHWH. They were condemned in no uncertain terms as the cause of compromises with idolatry and the wrath of God upon his rule. By and by they brought calamity.

13:2. Fulfilment of this prophecy is recorded in 2 Kings 23:16.

14:19 to 15:32. This passage is an extended historical record. The following facts show that it was used to prove the fulfilment of Ahijah's prophecy concerning the cutting off of Jeroboam's house: (1) the account of Nadab, the son of Jeroboam, is split as was that of Rehoboam; (2) the first part is given at the beginning, in 14:19-29, so as to introduce the question of the prophecy's fulfilment; (3) the second part is given at the end, in 15:25-32, and explicitly points out the fulfilment of the prophecy.

19:1-6. Ahab's account to Jezebel of the slaughter of the prophets of Baal evidently carried with it no restraint of Jezebel's determination to make Baal supreme in Israel. The fact of Ahab's submission was probably the cause of the great reaction in Elijah's feelings, leading to his expression of hopelessness under the juniper tree. Elijah's attitude toward Ahab immediately after the slaughter, and his going to Jezreel with him, indicate hope on his part that Ahab might yet be won for the Lord. At Jezreel his hopes were dashed by Jezebel's hold upon the king, and he fled. All this led to the giving up of Ahab and the naming of Jehu to be king over Israel. (Cf. 19:16.)

19:9-14. The manifestation of JHWH as "a still small voice" appears to teach Elijah that the quiet, seemingly weak influence of the Word of God has after all more power than earthquake and fire, or the violent forces of life. The earthquake and fire fit-

tingly describe such forces as those threatening his
life and the work of JHWH. They may also describe
such methods as he used to destroy the prophets of
Baal, but this is not certain. It is quite certain that
this experience was given of God to dispel his fear
of evil powers and to send him back into the thick
of the fight with plans for their overthrow. Directions about the anointing of Hazael, Jehu, and Elisha, which follow immediately, bear out this conclusion. This experience, accordingly, pays a majestic
tribute to the power of quiet teaching concerning
the will of JHWH.

21:17-26. This was the first direct announcement by Elijah of the utter condemnation of Ahab.
Its force speaks for itself. This is the great utterance around which the whole treatment of the house
of Ahab is arranged.

22:4. The alliance of Jehoshaphat with Ahab is
shown to have been a tragic mistake. The influence
of Jehoshaphat as a whole was good, but this mistake led to terrible things. Reference is made in
22:44 to this alliance as one of the blots on his record. One result is observed in 2 Kings 8:18, where
it is said of his son that "he walked in the ways of
the kings of Israel, as did the house of Ahab: for he
had the daughter of Ahab to wife; and [and so] he
did that which was evil in the sight of Jehovah."
Another is revealed in the fact that his grandson was
with Jehoram of Israel when Jehu attacked, and so
he, too, was slain by Jehu. Another followed immediately when Athaliah, that daughter of Ahab and

Jezebel mentioned in 8:18, and the mother of the grandson killed by Jehu, tried to kill all the seed royal of Judah. (Cf. 11:1-3.) Her purpose was frustrated and destruction of the reigning line temporarily prevented by Jehoiada's preservation of Joash. Even the rescue, however, could not stop the degrading influences that flowed from this alliance. As soon as Jehoiada's guiding hand was removed, these subtle tendencies dragged Joash down. All this is evidence that their contagious corruption was steadily spreading among the people. Thus Judah went the way of Israel.

22:15. This first word of Micaiah was repetition of what the false prophets had said. (Cf. 22:12.) Remembering that the guard who had brought Micaiah to the king had told him what the others prophesied, we may understand this word as a quotation, spoken ironically. The reply of the king (Cf. 22:16) shows that he understood Micaiah as not yet having spoken in the name of JHWH. The word which follows in 22:17 and 22:19-23 is marked as the word of JHWH.

22:22. The description of the false prophets as "his prophets"—i.e., prophets of King Ahab—is very apt. The false prophets depended upon the king's bounty for a living and allowed themselves to be influenced thereby so as to prophesy to please the king rather than JHWH. In other words they were "professional preachers."

2:24. The cursing described here has the force of "making contemptible." It brings to the light and to judgment the character of its object. The character judged in this case is revealed by the mocking described in 2:23. Those who did it were not small children, but lads whose disrespect for the prophet meant scorn of his work and his God. It needs to be noted furthermore that this cursing was "in the name of Jehovah." The prophet simply invoked the judgment of JHWH so as to make evident the contemptible attitude of these lads.

DATES OF CANONICAL PROPHETS

Before and During the Captivity

8:23. The parallel passage, 2 Chronicles 21:11-20, tells in 21:16-17 of the destruction of Jerusalem by Philistines and Arabians, which is a matter of foremost importance in connection with the date of Obadiah's prophecy. Because Obadiah, in verses 10-14, may refer to this same event, Obadiah is listed as possibly being a prophet of this era, about 845 B.C.

11:17 to 12:3. The influence of Jehoida, the high priest, over Joash is so marked by 11:17 and 12:2 as to show that Jehoiada was the real ruler of the kingdom in the early years of Joash. This fact coincides with certain conditions in the book of Joel, namely, the absence of any mention of a king and a manifestation of deep interest in the Temple and priestly affairs. Therefore, Joel is listed as possibly prophesying in the time of Joash, about 830.

14:25. The mention of Jonah, the son of Amittai, definitely places him in the reign of Jeroboam II, about 800 or later. In case Jonah, the son of Amittai, of the book of Jonah, is the same Jonah, we have the events of that book placed.

The lives and ministry of all the following are linked with events recorded in 2 Kings 15-25. Except for Isaiah they are not mentioned by name in the book, but they are included in the reference of 21:10, "Jehovah spake by his servants the prophets." It is possible that one or several of them wrote Kings. We need to carefully relate them to the message of Kings and weigh their influence.

Amos also prophesied in the day of Jeroboam II, as shown by Amos 1:1 and 7:10. While Jonah appeared near the beginning of his reign, Amos evidently came near the close, probably around 760.

Hosea 1:1 shows that Hosea's ministry stretched from the time of Uzziah to that of Hezekiah. Therefore, we assign it to the period 750-725. Hosea's ministry in the Northern Kingdom overlapped that of Isaiah and Micah in the Southern by a number of years.

Isaiah's call came in the year that Uzziah died. (Cf. Isa. 6:1.) There is uncertainty as to this date. It probably fell in the period 740-735, but may have been earlier. Isaiah continued into the reign of Manasseh, which began about 698. Thus his ministry extended over forty years or more.

Micah 1:1 shows that Micah's ministry began in the days of Jotham and continued into the reign of Hezekiah. The period probably was 735-700.

The last four mentioned, Amos, Hosea, Isaiah, and Micah, form a group known as "the great eighth century prophets." There is no doubt about their approximate dates. Their teaching is outstanding. Their books, therefore, have attained to foremost importance in the thinking of students of all schools of thought.

After this great eighth century group, the voice of prophecy was silent for about three quarters of a century. Then we come to another important group, including Nahum, Zephaniah, Habakkuk, Jeremiah, Ezekiel, and Daniel.

Nahum prophesied the fall of Nineveh but said nothing to indicate an immediate prospect. He must be put some years before the actual fall. Its fall is variously placed in the period 612-607. Thus Nahum may be listed about 630.

Zephaniah 2:12-15 prophesies the overthrow of Assyria; so Zephaniah also must be listed in the Assyrian period. He probably belongs about 630-625.

Jeremiah's ministry began in 628, according to Jeremiah 1:2, and continued till after the destruction of Jerusalem in 586. He was carried by the last remnant into Egypt. Thus his ministry continued more than forty-two years. He was a contemporary of all others in this group.

Habakkuk prophesied concerning the Chaldeans or Babylonians, before they completely overran Judah, yet while their coming was imminent. His work may well be placed about the time of the death of Josiah in 609.

Daniel was carried as a captive to Babylon with the first group of captives about 605 B.C. (Cf. Dan. 1:1-3.) As shown by Daniel 10:3 his ministry continued past the third year of the reign of Cyrus over Babylon. That means that his ministry practically coincided with the period of Judah's captivity, 605-535.

Ezekiel was carried captive with the second group of captives, about 597, and began his ministry among the captives five years later, as shown by Ezekiel 1:2. According to Ezekiel 29:17, the prophecy at that point came twenty-seven years after his captivity; so his ministry at least covered the period 592-570.

The following is a table showing the names and dates for these canonical, or writing, prophets:

1. Obadiah	about	845 B.C.	7. Micah	about	735-700 B.C.
2. Joel	"	830 B.C.	8. Nahum	"	630 B.C.
3. Jonah	"	800 B.C.	9. Zephaniah	"	630-625 B.C.
4. Amos	"	760 B.C.	10. Jeremiah	"	628-586 B.C.
5. Hosea	"	750-725 B.C.	11. Habakkuk	"	609 B.C.
6. Isaiah	"	740-695 B.C.	12. Daniel	"	605-535 B.C.
		13. Ezekiel about 592-570 B.C.			

CRITICAL PROBLEMS

I

Problems of Chronology and Numbers

In both Kings and 2 Chronicles there is a problem in chronology which is quite obvious as soon as one compares the total of years given for the reigns of kings with the possible limits of the period involved. The limits of the various periods are substantially fixed by parallel events in Assyrian, Egyptian, and Babylonian history. The chroniclers of those nations used more exact systems for dates than the Israelites, and information from their records is used to fix the dates of the various periods. How then can the totals of years for the kings' reigns be reconciled?

Because sons sometimes reigned as regents, as Jotham after Uzziah was stricken with leprosy, we know that there are many possibilities of overlapping. There are also evidences of the use of round numbers. Close study of these matters warrants the belief that solutions would appear in such ways, if we had all the facts.

The question of chief concern for us is this, Does this problem affect the credibility of events described and the interpretation of them? There is general agreement that it does not.

In 2 Chronicles particularly there is a very difficult problem as to numbers, as in the case of Abijah's four hundred thousand men against Jeroboam's eight hundred thousand. No definite degree of probability for any solution has yet appeared. It is a problem to be listed with that of numbers in books like Judges as an unsolved problem.

Again arises the question of effect on credibility of the message as a whole. If, as critics sometimes claim, these are examples of pious fraud, by which writers sought to make impressive their accounts of this history, then they do reflect seriously upon the motives and character of the authors. In such case, we must be inclined to accept one's work only when corroborated by other evidence. On the other hand, the consistency of the message as a whole must be weighed against the questions about details. High ethical standards in other matters must incline a student to search for explanations in copyist's errors, misunderstood circumstances, or idiomatic use of words now lost sight of.

Parallel Reading concerning this problem:

> Mack, Edward, "Chronology of the Old Testament," in *ISBE*.
>
> Curtis, E. L., "Chronology of the Old Testament," in *HDB*.
>
> Smith, W. F., "Number" (Sections III and IV), in *ISBE*.
>
> Konig, Ed., "Number," in *HDB*.

II

Use of Literary Sources

A wide use of sources is indicated. Some of them appear now as parts of the Old Testament canon. Many have disappeared. There are references to literary works other than those used as sources. It is clear that the authors had a considerable library and a well-developed literary background. The question as to how they used their sources, whether conscientiously or not, becomes not merely interesting but important in its bearing upon other problems.

Lists of these sources can be found in articles on Chronicles. Examination of their use constitutes a far-reaching project in criticism of the Bible. Do the transcriptions and editorial revisions indicate discriminating and trustworthy use of sources? This is too big a question to handle hastily. It seems, however, not too much to say that general appearances indicate an affirmative answer.

III
Book of the Law

The reference in 2 Kings 22:8 to "the book of the law" has been used by supporters of the Graff-Wellhausen Hypothesis concerning the origin of the law so as to date much of the legislation recorded in Deuteronomy in the time of Josiah. Conservative scholars have rejected such theories.

If it could be proved that Deuteronomy was written around 621 B.C. rather than in the time of Moses, the credibility of biblical history would be affected in all directions. Many points in Kings and Chronicles would appear in decidedly different light. Much that we see now as great examples of prophetic faith would have to be looked upon as manufactured history. Students ought to examine all such theories with utmost care before allowing their thinking to be altered by them. Exacting, thorough, conscientious criticism of such problems should never be avoided. Truth must be accepted no matter what preconceived ideas it uproots. However, tremendous efforts by scholarly men at this point have failed to remove the ground for confidence in the trustworthiness of the oldest Scriptures. Today there is also a trend of evidence from fields of study like archeology and comparative philology toward their confirmation.

Parallel reading: Rule, U. Z., "Law in the Old
Testament" (Sections II-1, 4), in *ISBE;* Orr, James,
"Criticism of the Bible" (Section III), in *ISBE;*
Easton, B.S., "Criticism (Graff-Wellhausen Hy-
pothesis)" (Section III), in *ISBE;* Driver, S. R.,
LOT, pp. 77-91; Orr, James, *POT,* pp. 256-262.

ARCHEOLOGICAL SIDELIGHTS

I

Comparative Value of Archeology and Prophecy

Many archeological sidelights appear in studies
of Kings. They do a great deal to confirm the historical records of the book. They are very valuable
as means of verifying and supplementing the historical narratives.

The prophecy, however, is the main theme of
Kings rather than the history. Those who would
keep the biblical emphasis cannot afford to forget
this. They cannot afford to let the unearthed ancient
life supplant the biblical emphasis on the faith of
the prophets. Archeology seems to have little opportunity to go beyond bare history. As a science,
it is not expected to do so. Prophetic faith is not
properly a part of a purely scientific study of antiq-
uities. The simple fact that prophetic faith deals
with future fulfilment of promises and archeological
science with data concerning the past makes them
to a great extent mutually exclusive. Prophets did
use history to support their faith. So may preachers of the gospel use archeology as a buttress. At the
same time the prophets always kept their gospel of
faith in JHWH as their dominating theme. So do

preachers of the gospel in all times need to appreciate the faith of the prophets, to emulate the faith of the prophets, and to propagate the faith of the prophets. Prophetic spirit will make them more than timid apologists for the past. Prophetic faith will make them triumphant inspirers of faith in God and hope for the future.

Parallel Reading:

Price, Ira M., *MOT,* (Sections 185-245.)

THEOLOGICAL STUDIES

I

The Message of Prophecy

Prophecy, in Kings, takes command over the destiny of the kingdom. Whereas in Samuel prophecy was a companion to jurisprudence and statecraft, acting in the role of interpreter and councilor concerning the establishment of the kingdom, it is forced in Kings to condemn the rulers and declare the taking away of the kingdom. Thus prophecy comes here to be the dominant influence. We must needs concentrate upon it in an effort to understand its meaning at this eventful time.

Seeking to analyze and appreciate this great, spiritual feature of the history of Israel, we shall observe first its prominent elements, then its main purposes, and finally certain distinctive characteristics.

1. Prominent Elements. Probably the most prominent elements are predictions, miracles, theological interpretations, and ethical teachings. These

terms are used to describe the prominent elements as seen from the human side. The human side is the most obvious. The divine side, however, is the most important for an understanding of Scripture. We must needs seek to see the relations of the two as Scripture gives them.

(1) The predictions mark prophecy as inspired by God. Accordingly the prophets are messengers of God.

In many unmistakable ways, apart from the mere attachment of God's name, these predictions evince their claim to be the Word of God.

They deal with far distant events. The foretelling of the end of the various dynasties does so in each case. There are also matters like the naming of Josiah, about three hundred years before his time, as the one to desecrate the altar at Bethel; the naming, probably twenty years before the time, of Jehu to be king of Israel and Hazael to be king of Syria; and the naming of Babylon, practically a century before the time, as the place of Judah's captivity. Such statements force us either to discredit the records of which they are a part as falsified interpretations of history, the work of deluded fanatics, or else accept them as words of God. Nothing lacking the inspiration of God's omniscience could see so far.

They deal with minute details. The rending of the kingdom in the days of Solomon's son, the cutting off of the houses of Jeroboam and Ahab in the days of their sons, and the reign of Jehu's sons to the fourth generation are very definitely specified.

If, however, one tends to think of these as predicted merely "on general principles," let him consider the death of Jeroboam's sick child at the moment of his mother's return, the killing by a lion of the man of Judah who prophesied against the altar at Bethel, the licking of Ahab's blood by dogs, the casting of Jehoram's body in Naboth's vineyard, the eating of Jezebel by dogs, and the continuance of Hezekiah's life for fifteen years. Nothing short of the wisdom of God could forecast and fulfil such details.

They deal with great affairs. The taking away of the kingdom in seven successive stages is the greatest matter of all. In addition there are matters like Ahab's two victories and Joash's three victories over the Syrians, the extension of Israel's borders by Jeroboam II, and the destruction of Sennacherib's host. Mere chance and imagination make no reasonable explanation for the prediction of such matters. There must needs be rejection as blasphemous claims of divine guidance or acceptance as accomplishments of God's Word.

They deal with laws of nature not subject to man's control. The happenings involved include the drought in Elijah's day and its breaking, the feeding of Elijah beside the brook Cherith and in the home of the widow of Zarephath, the increase of a widow's oil to relieve her debt according to Elisha's word, the coming of a son to the Shunammite woman, the cure of Naaman's leprosy, the inflicting of Naaman's leprosy suddenly upon Gehazi, and the recovery of Hezekiah from a fatal malady. If the announcement of such miraculous events lacked the support of the power of God, the announcement must have brought discredit as soon as time for proof had passed.

(2) The miracles marked prophecy as supported by the power of God.

Miracles and predictions are frequently associated so closely as to leave no occasion for distinction between the miraculous nature of the two. However, we use prediction here as the mere announcement of future events, and miracle of events so clearly extraordinary as to be recognized by the people generally as due to supernatural causation.

Many passages show that miracles were accepted as evidence of God's support. Now and then the conviction is stated. Concerning the feeding of Elijah by the widow of Zarephath, it is written, "The jar of meal wasted not, neither did the cruse of oil fail, according to the word of Jehovah." When Elijah raised the widow's son, she said, "Now I know that thou art a man of God, and that the word of Jehovah in thy mouth is truth." When asking for the fire to come down in his contest with the prophets of Baal, Elijah prayed, "O Jehovah, . . . let it be known this day that thou art God in Israel, and that I am thy servant, and that I have done all these things at thy word." When the answer came, the people fell on their faces; and they said, "Jehovah, he is God; Jehovah, he is God."

(3) The theological interpretations mark prophecy as instruction concerning God.

The subject of God is not taken up as a lesson and covered by systematic instruction. On the other hand, experience is frequently interpreted as proving the existence, the presence, and the attributes of God.

The predictions and miracles are frequently pointed out as proofs of his existence and presence. References to the living God, to his hearing prayer, and his speaking to the prophets seem likewise intended.

Various attributes of his nature are referred to here and there. Solomon's prayer gives fine expression to his omnipresence, saying, "Behold, heaven and the heaven of heavens cannot contain thee;" and his omniscience, saying, "Thou, even thou only, knowest the hearts of all the children of men." Such expressions as "Jehovah, he is God; there is none else" are evidently intended to convey assurance of omnipotence as well as mere existence. Everywhere in the messages of the prophets the belief is obvious that his power overrules all experience, all peoples, all history, so as to fulfil his covenants. Emphasis is laid on his control of all so as to remain faithful to his promises. Particular attention is given to the fulfilment of promises to Moses and to David.

The attributes of his moral character are thought of as the principles according to which his government of the world is run. His lovingkindness, his faithfulness, or his righteousness furnish the motive in every case. His rule is rounded out finally by all of them. The circumstances and attributes of those with whom he deals determine which attribute moves him at some particular time, but in the end his whole moral character is to be perfectly satisfied. These teachings show that prophecy is grounded in the ethical monotheism of Moses. There are many reflections of its teaching as given in Deuteronomy. Prophecy thus becomes an historic application of ethical monotheism to the life of Israel.

(4) The ethical teachings mark prophecy as instruction concerning conduct consistent with JHWH worship.

The standards of right conduct are not allowed to depend upon mere conscience, human judgment, temporary welfare, political expediency, or any other man-made standard. Revelations of the character of JHWH are unequivocably maintained as the fundamental standard of what is right and wrong.

The condemnation of Solomon is carefully developed on this basis. In the very beginning his marriage to Pharaoh's daughter is mentioned without definite indication of approval or disapproval. Then his visions, works, and rewards are described. Sprinkled over the pictures of his wisdom, honor, and riches are facts which reveal the growing influence over him of this heathen princess. There is an increasing tone of warning in the revelations. Finally, full indictment comes, charging that the love of many foreign women led to flagrant idolatry and on to the rending of the kingdom. The conscience is taught to see that this marriage to Pharaoh's daughter was wrong, no matter what plausible excuses there may have been for it. Maybe Solomon thought he might win her to JHWH later. The deduction is that he ought to have won her before marriage or not to have married her. The most likely excuse in Solomon's mind was that affinity with Pharaoh would promote prestige, and peace, and trade. Such standards of conduct are exactly such as the ethics of JHWH worship disallow.

"The sins of Jeroboam the son of Nebat" were motivated by political expediency, but they are the very things accounted by the prophets as causing Jeroboam and all his successors to fail to be established as David. In the thinking of the kings their policies appeared necessary, yet those policies ruined their cause.

Judah was condemned on similar grounds over and over, especially that of trusting in alliances with foreign powers. She was finally cast off that she might learn in the crucible of suffering to trust in JHWH and him alone.

2. Main Purposes. All elements of prophecy are best understood when their relation to the main purposes are observed. These main purposes, as they appear in Kings, are to condemn sin, to encourage repentance, and to inspire faith.

(1) The condemnation of sin is the major of all objectives. Three notorious examples of sin are treated. They are condemned by predictions, by miraculous signs, by explanations of JHWH's will,

and by tracing of consequences. Their condemnation is extended till it largely fills the book.

The sins of Solomon are dealt with first.

The story as a whole is skilfully constructed to show why a fine beginning led to a bad ending. In the beginning miraculous visions of JHWH, prophetic encouragements to obedience, and personal appreciation of the ethical standards of JHWH combine to provoke a good response and great reward. Yet the sprouting, spreading, and spoiling of sin is revealed along with the glory. Condemnation is simply a climax. Though tragic it becomes evidently inevitable.

We see in this story, therefore, a reminder that prophecy is primarily intended to save from sin. It concentrates on condemnation only when disregarded. The comparatively overwhelming emphasis at this time on condemnation is surely due to the fact that sin prevailed. Because sin prevailed, the theme of the book is the taking away of the kingdom.

There is evidence also that predictions are based upon both reason and revelation. Ahijah's prediction of the split in the kingdom followed years of close observation of the ethical tendencies of Solomon. Revelations had given occasion for critical observation. The picking of Jeroboam as a leader was quite reasonable after all that. He had proved himself capable. He was well known. He belonged to the Ten Tribes which had come slowly into David's kingdom. He knew from experience the burdens and dissatisfaction of the people. Knowledge of all these facts doubtless prepared the mind of the prophet for the guidance which gave the germinal seed of the prophecy. Reasonable and prayerful consideration, as well as revelation, contributed to its conception. Conviction, as well as guidance, brought it forth.

The harmony of reason and revelation seems to be characteristic of all prophetical predictions. The preparation of the human ground through prayer and study is not always so apparent, but there is nothing to deny its existence anywhere. The naming of Josiah three hundred years before his time is sometimes thought to have had no occasion in the circumstances of the prophet. On the contrary, we need to remember how prone the Israelites have always been to use names as descriptions of character. Remembering then that this prophet was characterizing one who would destroy the altar at Bethel, we ought to ask ourselves, What sort of a name would we expect him to select? Surely he thought of this destruction as a move to save the people of JHWH. Surely he thought of the agent as one through whom JHWH would accomplish that salvation. Seeing that Josiah means JHWH Supports him, we find a very definite connection between the name and the prophet's probable thinking.

This means that we should never think of the predictions of prophecy as born of chance, fanaticism, or any sort of spiritual hypnotism. Such things are the marks of false prophecy. In other words, the words of the prophets are never the results of mere vaticination. They are fruits of spiritual persuasion but never of mechanical spiritual compulsion.

This means, moreover, that the same sort of spiritual guidance is available for children of God in all times as in this one. Their times, their needs, their prayers, their convictions may differ, but their God and the manner of his guidance does not change essentially.

This means above all that the same sort of spiritual guidance is available for all the children of God. Their use of it differs but not their access to it.

"The sins of Jeroboam, the son of Nebat," are condemned as the cause of the woes of the kingdom of Israel from beginning to end. These sins of Jeroboam are detailed in the first passage describing his reign. Thereafter they are referred to like a text till the Ten Tribes go into captivity. Over and over and over these references occur. Each king is judged according as he walks in the ways of Jeroboam. Despite widespread reform, Jehu did not remove the golden calves and is condemned for that reason.

On the other hand, the condemnation of those led astray by these sins was never arbitrary. Over and over the prophets strove to save their kings from this condemnation. The most striking illustration is the word of Ahijah to Jeroboam himself, "If thou wilt hearken unto all that I command thee . . . I will . . . build thee a sure house, as I built for David" (1 Kings 11:38). The prophets seem to understand that such opportunity for blessing remains open to all those who rise to power. So Elijah

hopes to win Ahab and is bitterly disappointed by
Jezebel's victory over him. Unqualified condemnation did not come until the individual's own life
revealed his rejection of the promises of JHWH.

In the midst of this long, agonizing struggle with
the sins of Jeroboam, miracles attain to a prominence
probably equaled only in the times of Moses and
Jesus. We have, therefore, in this connection one
of our best opportunities to observe their use.

Many miracles are means of relief. Hunger, debt,
sorrow, and so forth are relieved. Doubtless the
prophet desired that such visitations of God's good-
ness would draw the hearts of men to God. No
other essential condition, however, appears at times
than pure relief. Surely we can agree that no other
is ethically necessary.

Many miracles are means of warning. Those
which are sometimes considered unjustifiably harsh
are to be classified here. When we remember what
scrupulous care is used at other times to make the
justice of JHWH to individuals clearly manifest,
we may reasonably suppose that such justice is not
violated in these cases. Add to this the fact that
instances are used as warnings, and we may reasonably conclude that all were so intended. Elijah,
calling down fire upon those identified with idolatry, was fulfilling his prayer, "that this people may
know that thou, Jehovah, art God." Elisha, cursing
the mocking lads from Bethel, may be understood
as making an example of them to all those so identified with idolatry as to deride the prophet of JHWH.

The ethical justification of these harsh measures is supported with tremendous power by a study of the moral conditions prevailing in these times. Examination of the contaminating and damning influence of Jezebel and her daughter Athaliah will make these conditions lurid. The spread of the licentious degradation of Baal worship among the people is tragically reflected in the experience of Hosea. The wholesale corruption of prophets, priests, and princes, that makes the nation's leadership an abomination in JHWH's sight, is abundantly illustrated in all the books of the prophets. Even so, the prophets had need to command respect for the Word of God in the face of scorn, persecution, and blasphemous denial of their divine commission. Often they had to do so alone and undefended except by God. Facing these emergencies, their God worked miracles in answer to their prayers.

At the same time, it helps greatly to observe that these were temporary measures. The appearance of JHWH to Elijah on Mount Sinai, not in the earthquake, and not in the fire, but as a "still, small voice," taught him to depend instead on quiet, patient instructions. He was sent back into the struggle to find a successor for himself in Elisha and to prepare the way for Jehu and Hazael. Elisha did much to help "the sons of the prophets," men gathered for prophetic instruction. He mingled with the people, cultivating helpful, friendly relations with the high and the low, teaching about God. The writing prophets arose ere long to carry on by dependence upon the written word. In a thousand ways and times the still, small voice of God has continued through the ages, as compared to scattered emergency uses of the miraculous.

The sins of Manasseh were condemned by the prophets as a third notorious example of sin. Though Josiah's great reforms followed Manasseh, these prophets said, "Notwithstanding, Jehovah turned not from the fierceness of his great wrath, . . . because of all the provocations wherewith Manasseh had provoked him" (2 Kings 23:26. Cf. 2 Kings 21:10-15).

The doom of Judah had been predicted by Isaiah and Micah long before this word concerning Manasseh. Why, then, is responsibility laid upon Manasseh? The only answer there can be is that no man is condemned for the sins of his fathers, even as Jeremiah and Ezekiel came to teach a little later. When Hezekiah prayed, he was spared. When Josiah honored JHWH, he was honored. When Manasseh grievously sinned, his kingdom was marked as doomed.

Another important observation concerning prophecy arises out of the facts cited in the preceding paragraph. The predictions of prophecy are certain but never unconditional. The rending of Solomon's kingdom was certain when Ahijah predicted it but not till conditions fully warranted it was it fulfilled. The cutting off of Israel's rulers was certain in any and every instance of prophetic proscription but never fulfilled till all conditions of penitence, attempted reform, and final failure were finished. The exile of Judah was certain that very day Isaiah told Hezekiah it would come to pass in Babylon, but it came to pass only after there were no more Josiahs to delay it. These facts are of utmost importance to the ethical perfection of JHWH's dealing with his people and sorely need to be more clearly recognized by us. Commentators frequently use inconsistent descriptions of these matters even when their intentions appear sound.

Another very helpful observation arises here concerning JHWH's providential dealing with Josiah. Even his death is seen as a providential blessing. He died fighting for what he believed right. His body was brought back home and buried with honor. Moreover, he was not there to see the terrible things that swept over his people very shortly thereafter. Accordingly, there was fulfilled the prophecy of Huldah based upon the newly discovered Book of the Law. Also a word from Isaiah (57:1) received an historic example of fulfilment:

"The righteous perisheth, and no man layeth
    it to heart;
and merciful [godly] men are taken away,
    none considering
that the righteous is taken away from the
    evil to come."

(2) The encouragement of repentance comes as often as there is occasion.

All delays in execution of sentences of doom should be understood as opportunities for repentance.

Every move in the direction of repentance seems to have been met with encouragement. When Jeroboam I asked for restoration of his withered hand, the prophet prayed that his request be granted and was heard. Even Ahab's penitence following Elijah's fearful castigation of him in Naboth's vineyard was met by postponement of the full punishment.

(3) The inspiration of faith was of course the chief desire of the prophets.

There is typical satisfaction shining through the words of Isaiah as he assures Hezekiah of the answer to his prayer for deliverance from Sennacherib.

Huldah's word to Josiah concerning the Lord's reward for his repentance and faith shows how true the prophetic message was to the deserts of the faithful, even in the days of impending and complete dissolution.

The fact that the weight of the prophetic message in Kings is on sin and condemnation rather than on faith and restoration can be readily seen as due to the trend of its time. Restoration is left to the various books of the prophets.

3. Distinctions Between True and False Prophecy. Arising out of these facts about prophecy, certain characteristics appear which distinguish true prophecy. In fact, these characteristics indelibly mark the message of men of God, preachers of right-

eousness, in all times. They are loyalty to previous revelation, practical and immediate effort to save souls from sin, and evangelical hope in the establishment of the kingdom of God.

(1) Loyalty to previous revelation meant loyalty to the promises unto David. They were used as a basis for appeals to Solomon and to Jeroboam. Again it meant, in the case of Huldah, loyalty to the Book of the Law. In all cases it meant loyalty to the words of previous prophets. Regularly a prophet builds upon the work of predecessors, then brings some contribution of his own. A very profitable study for us, therefore, is to weigh the message of each so as to identify distinctive contributions and line them up that they may point us to the lessons touching our day and our future. No preacher of Scripture can consider himself thoroughly prepared for his responsibilities till this is done. Also it follows that anyone disloyal to previous revelation is branded thereby as a false representative of the God of the Bible.

(2) Practical and immediate effort to save souls from sin is the supreme concern of prophets touching their own time and their own people. This passion made the distinction between Micaiah and the false prophets who deceived Ahab. Those false prophets were more interested in the king's favor and bounty than in his sinful condition. There were many others who knew the truths of previous revelation but did nothing to bring those truths to

bear on the lives of their fellows. That is the main reason why they were not prophets.

(3) Evangelical hope in the establishment of the kingdom of God means that prophets do not lose hope despite the many, long, bitter disappointments they face. At times their hope goes into eclipse, as did that of Elijah under the juniper tree. But, God brings them into experiences like that of Elijah at Sinai, and the still, small voice sends them back to face their work with an undying hope. JHWH promised Abraham and David to establish the kingdom in their seed; and, no matter what men or women do to spoil it, no matter what ages tend to dim it, still they believe it is coming. Yea, they make that hope an evangel to keep alive the faith of a remnant, like the seven thousand of Elijah's day that had not bowed the knee to Baal. Thus they seek to know the future, not to satisfy idle curiosity, not to build intellectual pride, not to give vent to vengeance, but to build the kingdom of God.

Conclusion

Prophecy kept alive the promises of JHWH concerning the kingdom despite every taking away of the kingdom. Even so, it built up a glorious messianic hope of restoration. The story of Messiah is not the story of Kings, but it is told by the same messengers of JHWH whose messages make the book of Kings. Prophecy in Kings did pave the way for prophetic revelations of Messiah, making evident the necessity for such a Saviour, and creating a hunger of soul for such a Saviour.

Parallel Reading:

Orelli, C. Von, "Prophecy, Prophets," in *ISBE*.

Davidson, A. B., "Prophecy and Prophets," in *HDB*.

Farrar, F. W., *The Minor Prophets*, chaps. I and IV.

Robinson, T. H., *Prophecy and Prophets*, chaps. I-IV.

Kirkpatrick, A. F., *Doctrine of the Prophets*, Introduction.

Beecher, W. J., *The Prophets and the Promise*.

INTRODUCTION TO PROVERBS

Parallel Reading

Genung, J. F., "Book of Proverbs," in *ISBE*.
Nowack, W., "Book of Proverbs," in *HDB*.
Driver, S. R., *LOT*, chap. VIII.

Name

The name "Proverbs" is derived from the first word of the Hebrew title. The singular of this word is *mashal*, a comparison, likeness, or illustration. A typical proverb appears in Proverbs 10:1:

"A wise son maketh a glad father;

But a foolish son is the heaviness of his mother."
This illustrates the general nature of a proverb as a "brief sententious saying." It illustrates also the classic literary form of the *mashal* which prevails in the book of Proverbs. This special form is a bit of literary artistry which uses the balanced statements of poetic parallelism in addition to compact wording and skilful expression. It sets two statements opposite each other by way of contrast, repetition, and supplement. Sometimes the form is extended to permit more varied expression, but the couplet is the classic form.

Date and Authorship

The present arrangement of the book was probably made near the end of Hezekiah's reign, before 700 B.C. The heading given in 25:1, saying, "The proverbs of Solomon, which the men of Hezekiah copied out," indicates this conclusion. There is nothing to indicate a later date for "the words of

[55]

Agur" in chapter 30 and "the words of King Lemuel" in chapter 31. The main part of the collection was probably arranged in Solomon's day.

Agur and Lemuel have already been noticed as authors of portions of the book. Two other portions, 22:17 to 24:22 and 24:23-34, are called "the words of the wise." Solomon is the only other author mentioned by name, but anonymous authors should probably be given credit for parts.

Method and Purpose

The whole book is a loose collection of proverbs. At times there is a general arrangement according to subjects. In chapters 1-9 the contrast of wisdom and folly furnishes a very general topic. In chapter 8, where wisdom is personified, she gives a close unity. As a rule, however, the couplet form of the *mashal* is used, and each one is such a close unit within itself that it does not encourage close relations with others.

The book does state a purpose that rules the entire collection. This is found in 1:1-6. In a word this purpose is to know wisdom (1:2), to receive wisdom (1:3), and to give wisdom (1:4-6).

OUTLINE
Illustrations of Wisdom
Title: 1:1
Statement of purpose 1:2-6
I
Pleas of Wisdom 1:7 to 9:18
Int. A contrast of the beginnings of wisdom and
folly 1:7

II

Collection of the Proverbs of Solomon. 10:1 to 22:16

III

"The Words of the Wise." 22:17 to 24:22

IV

Other Words of the Wise. 24:23-34

V

Other Proverbs of Solomon Copied by the
Men of Hezekiah. 25:1 to 29:27.

VI

Words of Agur, the Son of Jakeh. 30:1-33

VII

Words of King Lemuel. 31:1-31

TEXTUAL NOTES

Indications of Outline in 1:7 to 9:18

In 1:8 we come upon the expression, "My son," for the first time. It is the beginning of a plea to hear instruction. That plea continues through the first chapter. In 2:1 we find this expression again as the beginning of another plea. So it occurs in 3:1; 4:1, 10, 20; 5:1; 6:1, 20; 7:1. Thus it seems intended to mark a series of pleas of wisdom.

There are several other uses of the expression in this section, as in 3:21; 7:24; 8:32. Of course the use of the plural in certain cases is not considered a change in any essential sense. These instances are not listed with the first group because they are not used at the beginning of a plea. They continue pleas previously begun, and in the last two instances mark final, urgent forms of that plea. There seems to be nothing about them to dispute the conclusion that the other instances were intended to indicate the main divisions of this section.

If the foregoing be true, the purpose of one verse preceding the first plea and a whole chapter following the last becomes an interesting question. Observation of these passages shows that each gives a finely drawn contrast between wisdom and folly. The important difference between them is that the first contrasts the beginnings of wisdom and folly while the second contrasts their endings. How fittingly then does the simple *mashal* at the beginning serve as an introduction and the elaborate one at the end as a conclusion to the pleas of wisdom!

The loose arrangement of the book as a whole gives very little indication of the prominent topics. It is profitable, nevertheless, for the student to examine the individual proverbs according to topics, and to outline their teaching as far as possible for himself. To facilitate such study, outstanding groups are given below. The references and the subjects are not complete. Let the student add as he sees fit.

Purity

2:16-19; 5:1-23; 6:23-35; 7:1-27; 9:13-18; 12:4; 14:1; 22:14; 23:27, 28; 29:3; 31:3.

Work

6:6-11; 10:4-5,26; 12:11,24,27; 13:4; 14:23; 15:19; 16:26; 18:9; 19:15,24; 20:4,13; 21:5,25; 22:13,29; 24:30-34; 26:4,13-16; 27:23-27; 31:27.

Wealth

3:9; 4:7; 8:10-11,18; 10:4,15-16,22; 11:4,16,28; 13:7-8,11,21-22; 14:20,24; 15:6,16-17, 27; 16:8,16, 19; 17:2; 18:11; 19:1,4,6-7; 20:21; 21:6,17,20; 22: 4,7,16; 23:4-5; 28:6,8,11,16,20,22; 30:8-9.

Benevolence

3:27,28; 11:24-26; 14:21,31; 19:17; 22:4.

Surety Debts

6:1-5; 11:15; 17:18; 20:16; 22:26; 27:13.

Wine

4:17; 20:1; 23:20-21,29-35; 31:4-5.

Friendliness
12:26; 16:7; 17:17; 18:24; 25:17; 27:6,9-10, 14,17.

Use of the Tongue
11:11,13; 12:18-19,22; 13:2-3; 15:1-2,4,23; 16: 28; 17:14,20; 18:21; 20:3; 21:9,23; 24:26; 25:11.

Anger
14:17,29; 15:1,18; 16:32; 18:19; 19:11; 22:24.

Lying, Deceit, and Flattery
6:17; 14:25; 19:5,9,22; 20:17; 21:6; 25:18; 26: 19,24,28; 29:5.

Cruelty to Animals
12:10.

National Righteousness
14:34; 28:2,4-5; 29:4,12,14.

Family Relations
Value of a good wife: 12:4; 18:22; 19:14; 31: 10-31.

Contentiousness: 19:13; 21:9,19; 25:24; 27: 15-16.

Parental discipline: 1:8; 4:1-9; 6:20-22; 19:26; 22:6; 23:12-14,22-25; 29:15,17.

Parental blessing: 20:7.

Mutual benefits: 17:6.

CRITICAL PROBLEMS
IV

Solomonic Authorship of Proverbs
Many students of the book credit Solomon with scattered proverbs only, even in those parts bearing his name. The extent of his authorship is a prob-

lem, but the tendency to make his contribution a minor one or to remove from him credit for the character of the book seems unwarranted. 1 Kings 4:29-34 tells of intense literary activity in his day, and says, "He spake three thousand proverbs." Apart from definite indications within the book itself concerning the authorship of others, there is nothing to prevent our thinking of him as responsible for whatever it contains.

The use of Solomon's name at the beginning does not necessarily claim section 1:2 to 9:18 for Solomon. The words, "Proverbs of Solomon," appear again in 10:1. They seem, therefore, to be used at the beginning as a general title for the whole book. Inasmuch as their use permits indications of composite authorship at the end of the collection, it certainly does not preclude the possibility of such in the first section. At the same time it is possible that those responsible for the final arrangement of the collection took a production known to be Solomon's, yet without title, and put it ahead of the entitled Solomonic collection, because of its fitness to introduce all the works included. We agree that "fortunately we do not need to know the author of a wise saying in order to appreciate its beauty and accept it as a guide to conduct."[1]

The retention of the title, "Proverbs of Solomon," does certainly indicate a special connection between Solomon and section 10:1 to 22:16. The same may be said for chapters 25-29, the only dif-

---

[1]Sampey, J. R., *Heart of the Old Testament*, p. 130.

ference being that those in 10:1 to 22:16 were probably collected in Solomon's day. Concerning both it is possible to admit that the title may indicate nothing more than a type of proverb known as Solomon's. However, the use of similar titles in the same book to specify authors whose works include similar proverbs points strongly toward the use of this title to specify Solomon as the author of the proverbs in these sections. Of course he doubtless drew largely upon the sayings of his people and gave literary form to many proverbs already in use.

THEOLOGICAL STUDIES

II

The Contrast of Wisdom and Folly

In the first section of the book the contrast of wisdom and folly is pronounced. This accounts for the skilful arrangement of the introduction in 1:7 and the conclusion in 9:1-18. This contrast, though not so evident elsewhere, continues throughout the book. It furnishes a framework for the theological lessons of the whole book, relating all other topics to Wisdom and Folly as their beginnings, synonyms, and rewards.

1. Wisdom

(1)The beginning of wisdom

"The fear of Jehovah is the beginning of knowlledge" (Prov. 1:7a).

"The fear of Jehovah is the beginning of wisdom;

And the knowledge of the Holy One is understanding" (Prov. 9:10).

"The fear of Jehovah is the instruction of
wisdom;

And before honor goeth humility" (Prov. 15:33).

"Incline thine ear, and hear the words of the
wise,

.   .   .   .

That thy trust may be in Jehovah,

I have made them known unto thee this day,
even to thee" (Prov. 22:17a, 19).

This beginning, which is "the fear of Jehovah,"
is in 1:7 literally "the head thing of knowledge."
It is not an initial stage to be superseded by
something essentially different. It is a fountain
head from which all flows. It is a foetal head for
which a body is to be formed. It is a seed form
carrying in germinal state all the possibilities of
later development. It is faith responding to the
plea:

"Trust in Jehovah with all thy heart,

And lean not upon thine own understanding:

In all thy ways acknowledge him,

And he will direct thy paths" (Prov. 3:5-6).

Accordingly, repentance is implied, as in this:

"to the wise the way of life goeth upward,

That he may depart from Sheol beneath" (Prov.
15:24).

In the following repentance is definitely taught:

"He that covereth his transgressions shall not
prosper;

But whoso confesseth and forsaketh them shall
     obtain mercy" (Prov. 28:13).
This essential nature of the beginning gives point
to the injunction:
"Every word of God is tried:

     .   .   .   .

Add thou not unto his words,
Lest he reprove thee, and thou be found a liar"
     (Prov. 30:5a, 6).
The ethics of mere men is fatal because they
despise this essential beginning, even as it is said:
"There is a way that seemeth right unto a man;
But the end thereof are the ways of death"
     (Prov. 14:12).
The absolute necessity for a higher ground for
ethics than human judgment continues to be
stressed in 16:2-3; 21:2-3; 28:26.
Again we see all the teaching grounded in the
ethical monotheism of JHWH worship.
(2) The synonymns of wisdom
Probably the most important of all the synonyms
is the first mentioned, instruction. It is linked with
wisdom in 1:2-3 so as to indicate that they should
be construed as equivalent. It is constantly linked
with wisdom this way. We sometimes think of instruction as the act of instruction or the subject
matter of instruction. Here it appears to apply
more to the result of instruction. Thus it is training
or discipline. Where there is occasion for change, it
is correction. Where there is need for severity, it is
chastisement. All these meanings appear in Proverbs.

Discipline is the meaning of instruction which is most common perhaps. A few of the instances are 1:8; 4:1,13; 5:12,23; 6:23; 8:10,33; 13:1.

Correction appears in 7:22; 10:17; 15:5,10,32; 22:15; 23:13.

Chastisement appears in 3:11.

When we remember that the original idea of instruction includes all these terms, we realize that wisdom is not a mere explanation, not a mere offer, but an impartation. If we ask, An impartation of what? the question is answered by the synonyms which follow. Instruction describes wisdom both as given and as received. That is why it is an equivalent, paralleling wisdom throughout, while other synonyms are limited in one way or another.

Understanding, wise dealing, righteousness, justice, equity, prudence, knowledge, discretion, learning, and sound counsels all appear in 1:2-5 as synonyms of wisdom.

Reproof appears in 15:5,10,32.

Humility appears in 22:4.

The keeping of God's commandments appears in 4:4.

Mercy and kindness appear in 25:21.

Truth appears in 3:3.

Courage appears in 28:1.

The practice of any of the lessons concerning everyday affairs may be included. Important ones are those touching purity, industry, right use of wealth, benevolence, avoidance of security debts, anger, lying, deceit, flattery, cruelty to animals, friendliness, right use of the tongue, and national righteousness.

The highest of these synonyms is the giving of instruction, prudence, and discretion unto others. This is indicated in the statement of purpose. (Cf. 1:4.) The virtues observed before this do not necessarily rise above knowing and receiving. This one is the communication of wisdom by one soul to another. The following shows that it is more than impartation of knowledge through the written page:

> "Have not I written unto thee excellent things
> Of counsels and knowledge,
> To make thee know the certainty of the words
> of truth,
> That thou mayest carry back words of truth to
> them that sent thee" (Prov. 22:20-21).

Repeated illustrations come in advice concerning parental discipline. Examples appear in 13:24; 25: 12; 27:6; and 28:23. The comparison of a father's chastisement to that of JHWH in 3:12 is the finest of all:

> "My son, despise not the chastening of Jehovah;
> Neither be weary of his reproof:
> For whom Jehovah loveth he reproveth,
> Even as a father the son in whom he delight-
> eth" (Prov. 3:11-12).

(3) The rewards of wisdom

The idea of reward is clearly put in 23:17-18:

> "Let not thy heart envy sinners;

But be thou in the fear of Jehovah all the day
 long:
For surely there is a reward;
And thy hope shall not be cut off."

This idea of reward is illustrated in the house
wisdom builds and the feasts to which she invites.
(Cf. 9:1-6 and 24:3-4. It is also marked in 25:21-22
and in 28:10.)

A great list of specific rewards appears, including
the following: increase in learning and sound counsels in 1:5; security and quietness in 1:33; preservation in 2:8; understanding in righteousness and justice and equity, yea every good path, in 2:9;
pleasure in knowledge in 2:10; deliverance from the
evil way and evil men in 2:12; deliverance from
the strange woman in 2:16; dwelling in the land in
3:2; favor in sight of God and man in 3:4; providential guidance in 3:6; health in 3:8; prosperity in
3:10; happiness in 3:13; riches and honor in 3:16;
peace in 3:17; life unto thy soul in 3:22; confidence
in 3:26; grace in 4:9; wisdom in ruling in 19:12;
20:2,8,28; 21:1; 25:1-7; 31:4,5; atonement in 16:1;
life, righteousness, and honor in 21:21; a good name
in 22:1; riches, honor, and life in 22:4; mercy in
28:13; a prudent wife in 18:22, 19:14 and 31:10-31.

In many instances wisdom is the reward of wisdom. This fact reminds us of Jesus' word: "For
unto every one that hath shall be given, and he shall
have abundance: but from him that hath not, even
that which he hath shall be taken away" (Matt.
25:29).

2. Folly

(1) The beginning of folly.

"The foolish despise wisdom and instruction" (Prov. 1:7b).

"The way of a fool is right in his own eyes" (Prov. 12:15a).

"He that trusteth in his own heart is a fool" (Prov. 28:26).

Folly is thus described as the opposite or contradiction of wisdom. In modern theological terms it begins in unbelief, self-will, or pride.

(2) The synonyms of folly

Folly is lying in wait for blood and lurking privily for the innocent without cause in 1:11; robbery in 1:13; backsliding and carelessness in 1:32; perverseness, crookedness, and waywardness in 2:15; scoffing in 3:34; eating the bread of wickedness and drinking the wine of violence in 4:17; haughtiness, lying, and murder in 6:17; wicked purposes and mischief in 6:18; false witness and sowing of discord among brethren in 6:19; pride, arrogance, and perversity in 8:13; hatred in 10:12; shame in 11:2; transgression of the lips in 12:13; vexation in 12:16; speaking rashly in 12:18; sloth in 12:24; contention in 13:10; despising a father's correction in 15:5; desire for evil in 21:10; loving pleasure, wine, and oil in 21:17; hypocrisy in worship in 21:27; drunkenness and gluttony in 23:21; promoting one's own glory in 25:27; conceit in 26:11; self-praise in 27:2; jealousy in 27:4; greed in 28:25; stubbornness in 29:1; slander in 30:10.

The following passages sum up the meaning of folly in a way to make it detestable:

"The thought of foolishness is sin;
And the scoffer is an abomination to men"
(Prov. 24:9).

"As a dog that returneth to his vomit,
So is a fool that repeateth his folly"
(Prov. 26:11).

(3) The rewards of folly

The principle controlling the rewards of folly is expressed in 1:31:

"Therefore shall they eat of the fruit of their
own way,
And be filled with their own devices."

Other descriptions of the principle are found in 16:18; 19:29; 24:20; 26:27; 28:10.

Specific results are calamity, distress, and anguish in 1:27; disease in 5:11; falling and destruction in 16:18; judgment and stripes in 19:29; death in 21:16; despoiling in 22:23; poverty in 6:10-11; 23:21; 24:30-34; 28:19; dissipation in 31:3; cursing in 28:27; and destruction without remedy in 29:1.

No fitter conclusion could be formed, doubtless, than these words in 13:13:

"Whoso despiseth the word bringeth destruction on himself;
But he that feareth the commandment shall
be rewarded."

INTRODUCTION TO ECCLESIASTES

Parallel Reading

Beecher, W. J., "Ecclesiastes, or, The Preacher," in *ISBE*.

Peake, A. S., "Ecclesiastes," in *HDB*.

Driver, S. R., "Ecclesiastes," in *LOT*.

Name

The name "Ecclesiastes" is the Latinized form of the Greek translation of "the Preacher," which appears in 1:1-2, 12 and elsewhere.

Date and Authorship

The description of the Preacher as, "the son of David, king in Jerusalem," led to the opinion during many centuries that the author was Solomon. However, a large majority of modern scholars have concluded that this indicates merely that the author impersonated Solomon, interpreting the lessons drawn from Solomon's experience. By these the date is put between 440 and 200 B.C. Many things in vocabulary and syntax are said to prove the late date.

The question of date and authorship need not seriously affect the interpretation, for the book is true to the historical accounts of Solomon.

Purpose and Method

The message is developed through the book as a whole and reveals the author's intention to recite vain experiences and skepticisms so as to warn others against them. The book undoubtedly describes experiences that were sinful, but not that they should be emulated. It clearly delineates doubt in the mind of the Preacher, but not with the desire to propagate it. Each part must be judged in the light of the whole, as leading to the conclusion, "this is the end of the matter: all hath been heard: fear God, and keep his commandments; for this is the whole duty of man" (12:13).

OUTLINE

Vanities of Earthly Life
Title: 1:1

---

[1]This and other passages are marked with parentheses because of their parenthetical nature and the fact that taken together they form an important feature of the book.

(1) Concerning God's control of life 2:24-26
God gives a livelihood with happiness,
as the best in life, to those who please
him.

God gives travail to sinners.

(2) Concerning the relation of God's
control to man's purposes 3:1-15
God sets "a time for every purpose"
so as to make everything beautiful in
its time.

God sets inescapable travail in this life
and also eternity in man's heart that
man may discover that what God is
working out through it all is a purpose
to make man fear him.

5. Wickedness in high places makes men
to die as beasts die...................3:16-22
6. Power is on the side of oppressors.......4:1-3
7. Success breeds envy and strife..........4:4-6
8. Striving after riches brings lonely dissatisfaction 4:7-12
9. Old people, though kings, are soon
deserted 4:13-16
( ) Exhortations 5:1-9
(1) Not to make rash promises to God
or man 5:1-7
(2) To be patient with the king's execution of justice 5:8-9
10. Increase of goods brings increase of de-
pendents and sleeplessness to the owner
...................................5:10-12

11. Sudden loss of riches brings vexation, sickness, and wrath 5:13-17
12. Lack of power to eat destroys one's pleasure in riches, wealth, and honor.5:18 to 6:6
13. An uncontrolled appetite is never filled...6:7-9
14. Ignorance about the future increases vanity 6:10-12
( ) Exhortations to consider the end of things ....7:1 to 8:13
    (1) Of life 7:1-4
    (2) Of the mirth of fools...........7:5-6
    (3) Of extortion and bribery.........7:7
    (4) Of haste 7:8-9
    (5) Of adversity 7:10-14
    (6) Of excess 7:15-18
    (7) Of reproof 7:19-22
    (8) Of a woman's evil designs....7:23-29
    (9) Of a king's judgment..........8:1-8
   (10) Of a criminal's disregard for punishment 8:9-13
15. Similar fortunes and misfortunes for the righteous and the wicked......8:14 to 9:18
16. Little things that are bad, like dead flies in ointment, spoil great things that are good 10:1-4
17. "Folly is set in great dignity"..........10:5-7
18. Danger arises out of one's own work....10:8-11
19. Woe comes through foolish rulers.....10:12-20
( ) Exhortations to faith and hope....11:1 to 12:8
    (1) To take chances, doing good to others, in all kinds of times....11:1-6

TEXTUAL NOTES

1:2-3. Vanity is literally vapor or breath. This is why it is used in 2:17 parallel to "striving after wind." It describes that which accomplishes noth-ing, fruitlessness, worthlessness.

The statement, "all is vanity," must be under-stood in the light of the question in verse 3. The expression, "under the sun," indicates that the things called wholly vain are the things pertaining to earthly life. The return of the spirit to God, men-tioned in 12:7, and that which prepares the spirit for that return, are not included in this word. That return is the hope unto which the author would shut us up in his message, brought to a final emphasis in 12:8 upon the statement, "all is vanity." As great wing fences are built to guide cattle into a corral, so he stretches his warnings across all life to guide us into the fear of God.

1:4-11. The wearisome routine of all natural forces, going round and round so as to bring one back to the place of starting, says that earthly life begins with nothing, ends with nothing. This is the idea to be illustrated over and over throughout the book.

1:12-18. The word for wisdom in 1:13, 16-18 is understood here as synonymous with mere knowledge. The two are coupled in each of the last three verses.

There is a very important difference between wisdom here and wisdom in Proverbs 1:1-7. There wisdom is synonymous with knowledge that begins in the fear of JHWH. Here wisdom is synonymous with knowledge of "madness and folly" (1:17), and it serves only to make us realize that knowledge which does not lead to the fear of Jehovah is a vain knowledge.

2:1-11. Wisdom in 2:3, 9 is understood as mere experience of pleasure, or the knowledge arising from satisfaction of desire.

This wisdom is also quite different from the wisdom that accepts chastisement as a blessing. This wisdom that seeks the satiation of self-willed desires is far from the fear of JHWH.

2:12-17. Wisdom in 2:12-13 is understood as intelligence or sagacity. This saying in 2:14, "The wise man's eyes are in his head," indicates a shrewd use of knowledge. The wise man does not foolishly fail to use his eyes, as though they were not in his head.

Yet this wisdom is not necessarily rooted in the fear of JHWH. Its use of knowledge may still be utterly selfish. Then the wise man dies as the fool.

2:18-23. Wisdom in 2:21 is understood as success. In 2:21 it is made synonymous with knowledge and skilfulness. The word translated skilfulness means success. (Cf. note in *ASV*).

Even this sort of wisdom may not be grounded in the fear of JHWH. Then death requires the leaving of its fruits to another, and he may be a fool.

2:24 to 3:15. In this passage the author turns aside from his pessimism for the first time. He does so repeatedly as he goes on, gradually working upward to the great appeal at the end. Here he merely makes observations, but they are a logical foundation for the exhortations which follow.

Mistranslation of 3:11 seems to have stood in the way of clear interpretation of this passage. The *ASV* changed "the world" of the *AV* to "eternity," which is all right; but, it did not change the latter part of the verse, which is most confusing. Modern translations have not done any better. *MNT* not only continues the confusion at the end but also gives "mystery" for "the world." Smith's work on Ecclesiastes in *AT* resorts to a paraphrase of the whole which does not help.

A normal translation of the verse is, He makes everything beautiful in its time: also the ages (or eternity) he put in their hearts, without which man could not discover the work which God works from beginning to end.

These mistranslations of the latter part make it to have a meaning similar to the latter part of 7:14: "Yea, God hath made the one side by side with the other [i.e., prosperity and adversity], to the end that man should not find out anything that shall be after him."

The resulting similarity in translation has probably led to the failure to understand 3:11. However, the two differ decidedly in meaning. 7:14 is introduced by a conjunctive phrase, translated "to the end that." A more literal meaning of this phrase is "because of an order that" or "by reason of the fact." 3:11 is introduced by an entirely different phrase, the normal meaning being "because of the lack of which" or "without which." It is admitted by critics of the text that the customary translation of 3:11 gives a meaning to the introductory phrase not given to it anywhere else in the Bible, and that such odd translation renders the negative which follows pleonastic.[2] Nevertheless, they have persisted with that translation.

These two verses do not say the same thing, but they do supplement each other, and together they make clear the line of thought upon which the author builds his great exhortations at the end. 7:14 tells us that prosperity and adversity are mixed in human affairs according to an order of things fixed by the hand of God so that it is impossible for man to find out what will happen after he is gone from this life. The context of 3:11 and many other passages teach this same truth. 3:11 goes further and teaches us that God has also put in man's heart a sense of eternity, an expectation of the ages, including life

---

[2]Brown, Driver, and Briggs, *Hebrew and English Lexicon*, p. 115.

after this present; and that, without this hope of life beyond, man would not discover the work which God is working out through it all. The exhortations of 7:1 to 8:13, 11:1 to 12:8, and 12:13 make this work which God is working throughout this life to be the shutting up of man by means of death to recognition of the fact that the only hope he has for eternity lies in the fear of God. All this life is nothing, mere vanity. Therefore, let the sense of eternity save man from vanity and despair, helping him to find that which alone can make eternity blessed, the fear of God.

This interpretation makes the observations of 2:24 to 3:15 to be a fitting conclusion for the teaching up to that point. 1:12-18 teaches that the wisdom which is mere knowledge is vanity. 2:1-11 teaches that the wisdom which is mere pleasure is vanity. 2:12-17 teaches that the wisdom which is mere intelligence is vanity. 2:18-23 teaches that the wisdom which is mere success is vanity. Then 2:24 to 3:15 observes that God controls life so as to let the vanity of travail this side of the grave and the hope of eternity reaching beyond the grave shut man up unto one hope, the fear of God.

7:1 to 8:13. The central idea in this hortatory passage is most clearly observed in 7:1-2, 8, 14; 8:11-13, but it runs throughout. 7:1-2 make it clear to start with, advising the living to lay to heart lessons drawn from the day of death. Likewise all passages exhort men to consider the end of things. Superficial thought might take 7:14 as denying the possibility for such. But not so! Man is told that he cannot discover the life beyond before he enters it. But, this is told in order to advise him to consider God's purpose in making it so. This central idea runs through all passages.

11:1 to 12:8. This group of final exhortations appears as the goal toward which all the speculations, all the observations, and all the exhortations of the book have led.

The great passage in 12:1-8 is an artist's word picture of old age, the approach of death. Accordingly, 12:2 probably pictures loss of brightness or cheerfulness and the accompanying pessimism; 12:3 trembling of hand, stooping of shoulders, loss of teeth, and blindness; 12:4 isolation, nervousness, and lack of pleasure even in music; 12:5 fear of all sorts of little things; and 12:6-8 death itself. The purpose is to paint a background that gives unforgettable emphasis to this final form of the oft repeated warning about the end of earthly existence, "Remember also thy creator in the days of thy youth, before the evil days come."

THEOLOGICAL STUDIES

III

Vain Conceptions of Wisdom

Ecclesiastes presents several conceptions of wisdom only to brand them as vanity. It views with keen discrimination the objectives for which men have spent their lives in all ages only to come in the end to the same conviction with which Proverbs starts, "The fear of Jehovah is the beginning of wisdom." Moreover, it sees the fear of JHWH as "the whole duty of man." Thus Ecclesiastes deals chiefly with the negative side of wisdom, and Proverbs with the positive, the two together giving us a meaning for wisdom well reasoned yet spiritually defined. This negative treatment of Ecclesiastes first uses the word wisdom as synonymous with these vain conceptions; but goes on in a way to show that such are common ideas, worldly ways of thinking, vain definitions doomed to perish.

Thus knowledge, apart from the fear of JHWH, is vanity. Mere learning, and every philosophy built upon mere learning, is condemned. Every system of education not founded upon and kept true to JHWH worship is condemned. This has serious implications 'touching systems of state education which bar religious instruction.

Thus pleasure, apart from the fear of JHWH, is vanity. Selfish satisfaction of desire is condemned. Desire for the experience of evil ways, no matter how thrilling, informative, or aesthetic, is condemned. Every plan of man for business, government, public works, development of the arts, and so forth, which is contrary to ethical principles, is condemned. Every philosophy grounded on the natural plane only is condemned. Epicurianism is merely one of them. All that make development of the body and life for the purpose of selfish satisfaction are included.

Thus intelligence, apart from the fear of JHWH is vanity. This most subtle tendency of education, which encourages the idea that the educated have a right to use their cultivated intellect to get rather than give is spurned. All mere rationalism, trust in human reason unguided and unprotected by the divine, is cast out.

Thus success, apart from the fear of JHWH, is vanity. Every theory which magnifies sheer power is discarded. The thought that one can be ethically justified who uses opportunity, skill, or endeavor so as to require the maximum of service from one's fellows, and the minimum of benefit in return, is undermined. Every sort of materialism goes out.

INTRODUCTION TO SONG OF SONGS

Parallel Reading

Sampey, J. R., "Song of Songs," in *ISBE*.

Rothstein, J. W., "Song of Songs," in *HDB*.

Driver, S. R., "Song of Songs," in *LOT*.

Name

The name "Song of Songs" is taken from the superscription of the book. Some use Song of Solomon instead because the superscription adds, "which is Solomon's." Another name, "Canticles," is taken from the Latin translation of the first name. The name "Song of Songs" implies that this song is the choicest of all songs.

Date and Authorship

Many opinions have been advanced. Tradition points to Solomon. Critical theories have pointed sometimes to an author in northern Palestine shortly after Solomon, sometimes to the period just before the exile, sometimes to the time after the exile. Strong arguments are made out upon the basis of words used to the effect that it was not written in Solomon's time. It is clear that we do not know who wrote it or when. It is probable that "the book is about Solomon rather than by him."[1]

Method and Purpose

The method and purpose have been interpreted in three main ways:

1. As an allegory describing the love of JHWH and his people, or Christ and his church. In this case any sort of historical background is denied, the

---

[1]Sampey, J. R., *Syllabus for Old Testament Study*, p. 150.

composition is entirely a product of the imagination, picturing by dramatic fiction the fervor of religious faithfulness.

2. As a type used for the same purpose. Solomon and his bride are accepted as the speakers, but they are considered typical representatives of Messiah and his people.

3. As a literal love song, used to praise faithfulness in marriage. The method of the book, its lyric poetry, its dramatic spirit, and its vivid descriptions of physical charms are seen as a superlative example of the love songs which are customary parts of wedding feasts in Bible lands. The purpose, however, is interpreted as being upon a higher ethical plane than other love songs, as intended to rise far above mere erotic emotion and to demonstrate such faithfulness between lovers as is worthy of a place in the Scriptures. The Shulammite is seen as a beautiful country girl, brought by Solomon into his harem in order that she might assume there a queenly position, but who remains true to her shepherd lover. This faithfulness is seen as that praised in these words:

> "Many waters cannot quench love,
> Neither can floods drown it:
> If a man would give all the substance of his
>   house for love,
> He would utterly be contemned." S. of S. 8:7.

Many Jews and Christians have drawn spiritual inspiration from this song while interpreting it in one of the two first ways. There need be no quarrel

with those that do so, even if one is led to the conclusion that the author did not think of his own work
in the same way. However, the absence of even the
slightest intimation in his words that he thought of
what he wrote in other sense than the literal is very
strong argument for the third way of interpretation.
We may add the fact that the scriptures, old and
new, when they do use the marriage relation as a
type of the bonds binding believer and divinity, re-
frain from using detailed pictures of physical charms
as a part of their illustrations.

OUTLINE

The absence of indications as to who is the speak-
er at various places leaves the way open to divergent
interpretations. According to the theory of interpretation held, students differ widely and often concerning these points. It is doubtless best to leave
each one to work out his own according to his decision about the general interpretation.

THEOLOGICAL STUDIES

IV

Philosophical Attitude of the Wisdom Literature

In Proverbs, Ecclesiastes, and Song of Songs appears a type of literature known as "wisdom literature." Looked at as a whole, certain general characteristics appear in this wisdom literature which
help us to grasp its relation to other types of scripture teaching. These are its proverbial form, its
practical application, and its philosophical attitude.

The proverbial and practical aspects have been observed already, being fairly obvious. The philosophical attitude usually appears by implication only, and we are apt to overlook it. By doing so, one not only misses great lessons to be drawn from this literature but leaves the way open to appearances of contradiction and confusion.

A simple illustration of this implicit philosophy is found in the following:

"Answer not a fool according to his folly,
Lest thou also be like him.
Answer a fool according to his folly,
Lest he be wise in his own conceits" (Prov. 26:4, 5).

There is no contradiction or confusion. The very fact that such proverbs are put side by side shows that the authors sensed a general, universal, unifying ground of thought underlying all their sparkling sallies of wisdom, and took for granted that readers would exercise wit enough to do the same. This is evidence of their philosophical attitude. Making a parody on certain explicit philosophy in Ecclesiastes we may add:

There is a time to answer a fool,
And a time not to answer a fool.

The most explicit illustrations appear in Ecclesiastes. Its hortatory sections are characterized by their persistent advice to consider the end of things. In other words, this is advice to look at life as a whole or philosophically. This advice guides its condemnation of mere knowledge, selfish pleasure, unethical intelligence, and success ruled by the might-makes-right idea. This advice controls all its expressions of pessimism, leading to this majestic manifestation of spiritual courage and hope at the end:

> "Cast thy bread upon the waters;
> For thou shalt find it after many days"
> (Eccles. 11:1).

This advice controls all its expressions about death, sometimes seemingly skeptical as to a future life but leading to this sublime sermon at the end:

> "Remember also thy creator in the days of
>   thy youth,
> Before the evil days come,
> . . . .
>
> And the dust returneth to the earth as it was,
> And the spirit returneth unto God who gave
>   it" (Eccles. 12:1, 7).

All its teaching leads to the plea to fear JHWH. The fear of JHWH it calls "the whole duty of man." This circle of ideas forms a very definite philosophy. The emphasis upon the whole duty shows it to have been recognized as a philosophy.

Remembering how rich is the development in Proverbs of the positive and practical side of this "whole duty of man," we realize that we have a reasonably well developed philosophy. The wisdom literature does seek to deal with life as a whole. The theoretical side was not expounded in some one treatise so as make us think of it as a philosophy.

The philosophy of Israel was really its theology, the fear of JHWH, its ethical monotheism, expounded through all its scriptures. That is the unifying ground taken for granted in the proverbs noted above. That is the principle of universal consistency in every portion of Scripture.

The connection between this philosophy and the practical applications cannot be emphasized overmuch. All ethical relationships are pointed out as legitimate spheres of activity for JHWH worshipers. At the same time it is made evident that maintenance of the ethical principles involved cannot be sustained apart from unbroken faith in JHWH.

Ecclesiastes lays a basis for the inclusion of all phases of life in a godly scheme of things when it says:

> "For everything there is a season,
> And a time for every purpose under heaven;"
> (Eccles. 3:1)

and adds:

> "He [God] makes everything beautiful in its
>   time:
> Also he puts eternity in their [men's] heart,
> Without which man could not discover the
>   work which
> God works from beginning to end" (Eccles.
>   3:11).

Proverbs illustrates the application of this principle to everyday life. The Song of Songs illustrates its application to one vital phase of life, marriage.

Altogether these inspired examples of wisdom literature tell us that participation by JHWH worshipers in any endeavor which is an expression of the talents planted by God in human nature is proper so long as they fear JHWH. Society, business, politics, art, and many other fields, furnish opportunity for expression. Let the faithful never forget, however, that any and all of these will be vitiated if there cease to be continuous worship, exposition, and living of the principles of JHWH worship.

INTRODUCTION TO OBADIAH
Parallel Reading

Sampey, J. R., "Obadiah" and "Book of Obadiah," in *ISBE*.

Selbie, J. A., "Obadiah" and "Book of Obadiah," in *HDB*.

Driver, S. R., *LOT*, Chap VI, sec. 4.

Kirkpatrick, A. F., *Doctrine of the Prophets*, chap. II.

Name

The name Obadiah, as indicated by the first verse, is that of the author. It means Servant of JHWH.

Date and Authorship

We know nothing of the author beyond his authorship of the book. Other bearers of the name in the Old Testament give us no reason for identifying one of them with the author.

The reference in verses 10-14 to a destruction of Jerusalem is the only key to the date. So far as what is said in the book is concerned, it could fit either the destruction by Nebuchadnezzar in 587 B.C. or that described in 2 Chronicles 21:16f, which occurred about 845 B.C. Though critics are widely divided over these dates according to their views of language, unity, and relation to other prophetic messages, there is good reason, particularly on the ground of relation to other messages, for joining Orelli, Kirkpatrick, and Sampey in favor of the early date.

Method and Purpose

The destruction of Edom is the obvious theme. The method, however, is prophetic rather than his-

torical. One historical event is taken as occasion for
a prophecy. The purpose of the prophecy is not
merely to predict the destruction of Edom, but the
day of JHWH as well, the destruction of Edom being only a small part of the events of that day.

OUTLINE

Destruction of Edom

I

Decree: Complete Destruction 1:1-9

1. JHWH hath decreed it 1:1-4
   (1) Sending an ambassador to summons
       the nations against her 1:1-2
   (2) Her fortress cannot save her......1:3-4
2. The destruction shall be strangely terrible and complete 1:5-9
   (1) Worse than the work of thieves.....1:5
   (2) Carried out by her own confederates
       ....1:6-7
   (3) JHWH shall cut off every one of her
       wise and mighty men 1:8-9

II

Cause: Violence Done to His Brother Jacob 1:10-14

Int. Shame to cover Edom as a result of his
    unbrotherliness 1:10
1. Acting as one of Jacob's enemies when
   he was captured 1:11
2. Rejoicing in Jacob's distress..............1:12
3. Seeking benefit by Jacob's distress........1:13
4. Seeking to hinder Jacob's escape...........1:14

III

Time: Day of JHWH 1:15-21

1. When all nations will be destroyed......1:15-16
2. When Israel will be restored............1:17-20
3. When the Kingdom of JHWH will be
   established 1:21

CRITICAL PROBLEMS

V

Did Jeremiah Quote from Obadiah or Obadiah from Jeremiah?

It is not possible to cover critical questions in a summary treatment of interpretation. Study of some, however, leads to observations which enhance our appreciation of those teachings closest to the heart of the prophets. So it is in the comparison of Obadiah verses 1-9 with Jeremiah 49:7-22.

In addition to observations made in the required parallel reading, note the following: (1) Verses 8 and 9 in Obadiah predict the destruction of "every one" of the "wise men" and "the mighty" of Edom; (2) Jeremiah 49:11 points out hope for "fatherless children" and for "widows" who will trust in JHWH; (3) the passage in Obadiah leaves room for just such exceptions as are made in Jeremiah.

It may well be argued, as a support to the theory concerning Obadiah's early date, that the prediction of exceptions probably followed the general prediction. However, there is a point of far greater import here.

This is a fine illustration of the fact to be observed throughout the prophets that their supreme interest in the Day of JHWH was salvation of the remnants that trust in JHWH rather than the destruction of nations. They see them characterized by trust in JHWH. This it is that establishes the kingdom of JHWH. This it is that makes the kingdom of JHWH to be spiritual and universal.

THEOLOGICAL STUDIES

V

Day of JHWH

The most important part of Obadiah is its teaching about the day of JHWH. Not merely for the sake of understanding Obadiah, but also the swelling stream of prophecy which follows, we need to examine this day.

Origin of the Name

The first use of the name is here in Obadiah.

Antecedent ideas, however, appear far back in sacred history, with many connecting links.

The first evangel, revealed in the garden of Eden, recorded in Genesis 3:15, included the spiritual warfare of the human race and victory for a promised seed. That is the spring from which all these antecedent ideas flow.

The promises to Abraham, including cursing of those who curse him and blessing of those who bless him, are outstanding.

The blessing of Jacob upon Judah must be given great consideration. In Genesis 49:1, its fulfilment is described as coming "in the latter days." "The day of JHWH" is taken as one of the latter days. In Genesis 49:8-10, the fulfilment is described as including: (1) Judah's pre-eminence among his brethren; (2) Judah's rule "until Shiloh come," which is accepted as the advent of Messiah; (3) Judah's rule over all peoples.

The curses and the blessings, as outlined by Moses in Deuteronomy, are also features. Deuteronomy 30:1-10 sums up this teaching.

Connecting links are scattered all along in the words of Joshua, Samuel, David, Elijah, Elisha, and others dealing with the future of Israel and her enemies.

Outstanding Characteristics

Obadiah gives the outstanding characteristics with simplicity and clarity. We find the ideas of all succeeding prophecies touching this subject developed within the circle he draws. This and the word about Edom become his contributions to prophecy. The outstanding characteristics are:

1. All nations will be destroyed.
2. Israel will be restored.
3. The kingdom of Jehovah will be established.

Many of the prophecies recorded in Kings concerning the taking away of the kingdom preceded Obadiah. We are led, therefore, to the conclusion that his vision was intended to foreshadow the establishment through Israel's restoration of a new type of JHWH rule, one exceeding all previous ones in the degree of JHWH's presence and control. This new kingdom he called the kingdom of JHWH.

Supreme Hope

The day pictures the wrath of JHWH but also his favor. The preservation and restoration of the holy remnant, as mentioned in verse seventeen, becomes the supreme hope of the prophets for this day. To this they turn in their perorations, after dark and terrible pictures of wrath, to find words of hope expressing their optimistic, unquenchable, glorious faith in JHWH and the kingdom that will be when "the earth shall be full of the knowledge of Jehovah, as the waters cover the sea" (Isa. 11:9b).

INTRODUCTION TO JOEL

Parallel Reading

Robertson, James, "Joel," in *ISBE*.
Cameron, G. G., "Joel," in *HDB*.
Driver, S. R., *LOT*, chap. VI, sec. 2.
Kirkpatrick, A. F., *Doctrine of the Prophets*, chap. III.

Name

The name Joel, as indicated by the first verse, is that of the author. It means JHWH is God.

Date and Authorship

We know nothing of this author, as was also true of Obadiah, except what is stated in the book. The only historical fact given us is that he was the son of Pethuel, and that does not help us. There are many bearers of the name in the Old Testament, but no occasion appears for linking any other with the book.

There are no clear indications of date in the book. The only reasonably settled conclusion of critics is that the date is very early or very late in the period of writing prophets. The period 830-810 B.C. is accepted here as the probable date for the following reasons: (1) there is no consciousness of a king's influence manifested in the book; (2) priestly influence is strongly manifested; (3) these two facts fit in a peculiar way the time when Joash was young and Jehoiada the high priest was the virtual ruler; (4) the message of the book fits well between Obadiah and later prophets.

Method and Purpose

There is practically no narrative in Joel. The tiny bit in 2:18 is merely a steppingstone to a prophecy. The method is altogether that of prophetic address. The purpose permeating all the addresses is stress upon repentance. Bringing of Israel to repentance is shown to be the purpose of JHWH in the day of JHWH, and upon this repentance depend all future blessings.

OUTLINE

A Call to Repentance

(Title: 1:1)

Key verses: 2:12-13

I

II

III

Because Restoration Depends upon Repentance
2:12 to 3:21

THEOLOGICAL STUDIES

VI

New Views of the Day of JHWH

In the picture of restoration we find three distinctive contributions: (1) restoration depends upon repentance, (2) restoration will bring a pouring out of the Spirit, (3) restoration will occasion a time of judgment for all nations.

Dependence of Restoration Upon Repentance

To Obadiah's prophecy of restoration, Joel adds a powerful reminder that its spiritual condition is repentance. This colors all developments of the day of JHWH, giving to them an essential spiritual significance. All its punishments and all its blessings are determined according to this condition. We cannot understand them apart from this fundamental spiritual condition. Because of the fact that out of them arise most of the questions included in messianic teaching and modern eschatology, this is a matter of great importance.

Pouring Out of the Spirit

As the condition of restoration is spiritual, so the consequences are represented as a pouring out of the Spirit, a great spiritual fruitage. Upon all classes will come this blessing, men and women, young and old, servants as well as masters.

The fulfilment of this prophecy on the day of Pentecost, as pointed out by Peter in Acts 2:14-21, does not forbid other fulfilments.

Judgment for All Nations

This picture of the gathering of all nations for judgment is a decidedly new picture. By later prophets, however, it is greatly developed. The following features appear: (1) It is accomplished by JHWH; (2) It is caused by the unrighteous treatment of Israel at the hands of the nations; (3) It happens in time of warfare against Judah and Jerusalem; (4) It is climaxed by the miraculous intervention of JHWH; (5) It results in the purification of Judah and Jerusalem.

INTRODUCTION TO JONAH

Parallel Reading

Sampey, J. R., "Jonah" and "The Book of
    Jonah," in *ISBE*.

König, Ed., "Jonah," in *HDB*.

Driver, S. R., *LOT*, chap. VI, sec. 5.

Name

The introductory word in this case names Jonah
as the leading character of the story, not as the
author. It is Jonah's name, however, which is given
to the book. The description of him as "Jonah the
son of Amittai" corresponds exactly to that of the
Jonah mentioned in 2 Kings 14:25. The meaning
of the name, "A Dove," has no special connection
with the book.

Date and Authorship

Nothing is even intimated concerning the author
of the story as a whole. The poem in chapter two
is ascribed to Jonah. The possibility that Jonah
wrote all is not denied by the book. The possibility
that another put his story into its present literary
form is equally open.

Long and heated debate has gone on concerning
both authorship and date. The chief occasion is the
question whether the experience described is historical or parabolical. Suggested dates range all the
way from Jonah's time, about 800 B.C., down into
the interbiblical period.

Method and Purpose

The method is not ordinary historical narrative
or direct prophetic teaching. It presents the ex-

perience of Jonah in story form and dramatic style,
letting experience itself speak to the emotion, the
intelligence, and the will of all who read. It presents Jonah's experience in four stages and sees him
overruled each time by the providence of God so as
to be brought to acceptance of lessons which soar
to the height of spiritual outlook and missionary
responsibility.

The evident purpose is to present with compelling persuasiveness the responsibility of the saved
to save others. Let us remember that whatever experience Jonah had was passed on by him. No matter who gave it this dramatic form, the purpose of
the book is Jonah's purpose. No matter what littleness was in him to begin with, no matter how hard
it was for God to cure him, the purpose that glorifies this book glorifies the Jonah whose chastened
soul came back home to give to his own people a
vision of the spiritual nobility of missions.

OUTLINE

Making of a Missionary

I

Flight Prevented. 1:1-10

1. Fleeing from JHWH's call..............1:1-3
2. Caught by a storm...................1:4-10

II

Troubles Sanctified. 1:11 to 2:10

1. Willing to perish rather than preach....1:11-16
2. Brought to prayer by a fish........1:17 to 2:10

III

Hate Rebuked. 3:1-10

1. Preaching condemnation only 3:1-4
2. Refuted by JHWH's forgiveness of the
   Ninevites 3:5-10

IV

Love Inspired. 4:1-11

1. Displeased by God's mercy..............4:1-5
2. Taught a lesson in love by a gourd vine..4:6-11

CRITICAL PROBLEMS

VI

Is Jonah Historical or Parabolical?

If the book of Jonah is entirely the creation of its author, then the experience of Jonah is a mere parable. If the book uses experiences of the prophet and magnifies their significance by giving them dramatic, literary dress, then it is historical. The main point is in this question, Is Jonah of the book of Jonah the prophet who lived in Israel about 800 B.C. or a literary fiction?

The naming of this Jonah as "Jonah the son of Amittai," exactly as the prophet mentioned in 2 Kings 14:25 is named, must be weighed against critical theories which make this Jonah a mere fiction. These theories make the book of Jonah to slander the prophet Jonah.

The Aramaic expressions of Jonah do not settle the question. Galilee, where tradition places the birthplace of Jonah the prophet, was already experiencing strong influences from the Syrian people and the Aramaic language before Jonah's day.

New Testament references, particularly the implications of the words of Jesus, must be accorded supreme weight. Decisions concerning these will doubtless settle the debate for conservative students of Scripture. Passages for study in this connection are Matthew 12:29-41; 16:4; Luke 11:29-32.

We do well to remember as we ponder this problem that differences of opinion cannot destroy the teaching of the book. This is not to say for one moment that the question of historicity is not important, but merely to dispel discouragement in the face of contradictory opinions. The teaching of the book is so true to the spiritual experiences of God's children that its appeal cannot be destroyed by questions as to origin. What the message needs most is faithful, fearless presentation. It can take care of its own appeal.

THEOLOGICAL STUDIES

VII

Missionary Responsibility

The great message of Jonah is a missionary message. There are also valuable lessons concerning providence. To Joel's picture of repentance among Israelites, there is added a picture of repentance among the nations, telling us that they too may have a part thereby in the kingdom of God. All these lessons, however, are tributaries to the stream bearing the conscience of the children of God onto the wide ocean of responsibility for bringing others unto repentance and faith in JHWH. This great message brings Old Testament teaching concerning missionary responsibility to its highest point.

Selecting words from the book itself, this message of Jonah may be called:

Gourds or Souls

By the gourd vine at Nineveh, not in the fish, comes the climax of the story of Jonah.

What a tragedy it is that many of us follow Jonah into the fish and never get out! Jonah's experience in the fish led him to pray. When he prayed, God spoke to him a second time, saying, "Go to Nineveh." And he went! When we stand around Jonah's prayer room without getting down to pray for ourselves and for Nineveh, the spiritual danger signals are up. When we argue and argue whether or not the fish was a whale or some other sort of sea monster, whether or not a human body could withstand the decomposing powers of the fish's gastric juices for three days and three nights, without catching a vision of higher things, we miss a blessing of surpassing worth. When we allow the spiritual drama of those three days and nights to exhaust its powers of persuasion without our once lending a sympathetic understanding to poor Jonah's struggle of soul and without our pleading along with him for forgiveness, it is stark spiritual tragedy. It is appalling that many Christians have more interest in questions about the Bible than in carrying the message of the Bible to lost souls.

As Jonah goes to Nineveh, let us go with him. There, by the withered gourd vine, in view of a repentant and forgiven Nineveh, are the spiritual heights of the book of Jonah. There let Jonah and you and me stand together. The gourd is on one side, the souls of Nineveh on the other. JHWH says, "Thou hast had regard for the gourd, . . . and should not I have regard for Nineveh?" (Jonah 4:10-11).

JHWH's question to Jonah and to us is first of all a question of our selfishness versus the Lord's service. When Jehovah describes the gourd as that "for which thou hast not labored, neither madest it to grow," he makes us to see that this thing we desire for our own selfish satisfaction was provided by him, put into our possession and under our control by him in order that we might use it to help us serve him. Then he goes on to describe it as a thing that "came up in a night and perished in a night." Thus he sets its fleeting, temporal value over against eternal values.

I

Our Selfishness Versus the Lord's Service

This question deals with our providences, our possessions, and our passions. It touches all the pleasant things provided by the providence of God, but which we dare to consider private possessions, and which we allow to become occasions for destructive passions. It is a question of:

1. Our comfort versus the Creator's care for all.

"And it came to pass, when the sun arose, that God prepared a sultry east wind; and the sun beat upon the head of Jonah, that he fainted and requested for himself that he might die" (Jonah 4:8).

West winds came from the sea. They were moist and refreshing. East winds came from the desert. They were sultry and withering. In Jerusalem today the residents say to newcomers, "Never try to settle your differences while the *siroco* is blowing. Nerves are too apt to be on edge." As that wind continues to blow for one, two, three days, the leaves on the trees writhe and wilt and wither away.

Was it instead some morning at home when the thermometer climbed toward one hundred? Or, when the temperature dropped below zero? When floods came; the heating or cooling system broke down; mosquitoes, the baby, or visitors kept us awake; Sunday dinner needed to be prepared for kinsfolk, or we thought it did; we wanted a motor trip or a vacation? And we said, "Pshaw! The Lord cannot expect me to go to church today."

The Lord answers with a question, "Thou hast had regard for the gourd, . . . and should not I have regard for Nineveh?"

We do well to note in passing that this question does not imply a denial of all the claims of comfort. The Lord's servant, as often said, must be preserved in order to promote the Lord's service. He may want us to have time for rest, a good mattress, a good meal, steam heat, or an electric fan. He said, "Thou hast had regard for the gourd," and gave no rebuke for that phase of the matter.

On the other hand, he said, "Should not I have regard for Nineveh?" In other words, God says, If you see so clearly comforts you think I ought to provide for you, should you not see my concern for the salvation of others? If you see these little things and doggedly demand them, should you not be big enough to see the supreme concern of the Creator for the mighty mass of human beings he brought into being?

Again this question is a question of:

2. Our coveteousness versus the Heavenly Father's helpfulness.

Apparently, when that gourd grew up beside him, Jonah thought he had a claim upon it. It was in his possession, was it not? So he thought it belonged to him. Squatter's rights, maybe! And so, he would have fought to maintain his ownership had a fellow man disputed it with him. If that worm that cut it down had any longer been in sight, it would have have been too bad for that worm. To be sure, Jonah believed he had a right to the use of that gourd for his private pleasure.

Or, is the gourd now something given of God to us?

Is it a land, its produce, and its spiritual enlightenment, created by God; and, seeing that we want to keep these blessings for our private pleasure, we are unwilling to give of money and sons and daughters that other lands may share the gospel? Is it an inheritance of houses, business, or fortune, willed by parents; and, seeing that God lets depressions decrease them betimes, we say we will not believe in a god that does such things? Is it the opportunities of a land made rich by circumstances society has wrought out of the gifts of God; and, seeing that predatory foreigners look with covetous eyes upon it, we too become so shamelessly covetous that we resist in kind and protect our lives with nothing better than armies and navies? Is it a home, a school, a club, a fraternal order, whose culture, whose prestige, whose entertainment make us unwilling to give ourselves to mix with children, with the uneducated, with the underprivileged, with the "have-nots" of this world that they may have Jesus?

Again, JHWH's question implies the answer.

Again, let us note beforehand that the answer does not deny our right to use possessions, only our right to use them for ourselves alone. Property rights still stand. The use of property to produce values for mutual benefit is encouraged.

On the other hand, he said, "Should not I have regard for Nineveh?" Why should we feel our property rights so strongly and be unresponsive to the longing of God to conserve his rights in the souls he created? Is it not passing strange in us to see the values in possessions developed out of dirt and miss the values in persons made in the image of God? Is it not the height of folly to be so wise concerning earthly values and to despise heavenly values? Shame upon us to regard mere gourds more than souls!

Again the question is a question of:

3. Our hate versus the Saviour's salvation.

Jonah was very angry about the gourd. If he could have caught the worm that did the damage, dictionary words would never have sufficed to describe his language. As it was, he actually "talked back" at God. He said, "I do well to be angry even unto death."

Just what did make Jonah so angry? As is usual when people are sorely vexed by little things, there must have been something big behind it all.

Taking for granted that Jonah lived about 800 B.C., in the days of Jeroboam II, king of Israel, we know that in his day the Assyrians, the Ninevite armies, were pressing year by year closer and closer upon his beloved Galilee. Those armies were threatening to overrun his own people, his own native village, his own home and family. And those armies were as cruel as any ever known. The records of their kings, taken from their own national monuments, boast of horrors inflicted on captive populations to crush their resistance to the iron heel of Nineveh. Those things include the crucifixion of thousands of men before the eyes of their women and children, the flaying of the skin from the flesh of those yet alive, the impaling of men on sharpened stakes to die and rot as grasshoppers that a heartless boy has stuck alive upon a thorn. Moreover, those things were done as a matter of colonial policy, not as the uncontrollable outbursts of an army after battle, but as cold deliberate malice-aforethought, planned to extinguish every flicker of patriotic passion and perpetuate the ruthless despotism of Nineveh's mailed fist.

Like as not, Jonah felt that such people could not be saved. When he said, "I hasted to flee unto Tarshish, for I knew that thou art a gracious God, and merciful," he was thinking God would do, as he later did do, show mercy in response to repentance. At the same time, he was doubtless convinced that a profession of repentance by Ninevites could be nothing less than a sham, nothing more than "getting on the good side of God." He probably believed such people incapable of understanding JHWH's plan of salvation, unsusceptible to the spiritual influences that would generate a change of heart and life.

In a word, Jonah hated the Ninevites, and his hate blinded him to every hope for good in them.

Or, is it we who say, "A nigger ain't got no soul"? Is it we who say, "That damned Chink, or Dago, or Jew, or Greaser"? Is it we who think missions in Japan a fool's hope in view of her rape of China? Is it we who fear deep down in ourselves, whether we dare to say so out loud or not, that any form or fashion of messianic millennium is but a dream of those who are duped by religious fanaticism?

Still, as a "still, small voice," the question of God to Jonah implies the answer.

Once more we may note that it does not demand peace where there is no peace, compromise with the devil, or acceptance of evil as an inescapable necessity in this world.

It does imply a need to distinguish between the sinner and his sin. It encourages us to so hate the sinner's sin as to give ourselves to lead him to the Saviour's salvation.

II
The Temporal Versus the Eternal

JHWH turned his question to reflect another light when he said of the gourd, "which grew up in a night and perished in a night." We see the same things in a new light.

In this light the question is a question of:

1. Passing pleasures versus unfailing faithfulness.

Jonah wanted shade for a day. JHWH made his experience an example for eternity.

Apparently Jonah went back home and related his experience as a lesson to his people concerning their missionary responsibility. Else how could we have the book? Who could tell a story with such insights into spiritual experience without having been through it?

This lesson of the gourd vine becomes for all who see it a joy eternal. Thereafter selfish ease or satisfaction in the shade of a gourd vine becomes paltry and despicable.

In this light the question is a question of:

2. Perishing possessions versus unending usefulness.

Jonah stubbornly clung to a withered gourd vine. JHWH took it away and gave a spiritual service to all mankind.

One day a young preacher rode along a highway and observed a Negro man sitting beside the road. The Negro was of middle age and had a good face. He had taken off his shoes and was obviously tired, as from a long trip afoot. The preacher voluntarily offered him a ride. As they traveled the preacher said, "Sam, are you a Christian?" When no answer came the preacher looked at the Negro and found a surprised and wondering expression on his face. Finally he said, "Boss, you de fust white man eber axed me dat question."

God forbid that Southern white people think only of the money they can make out of their Negro neighbors. Otherwise, we may hear them say before God, "No man cared for my soul."

In this new but unfading light the question is a question of:

3. Unlimited littleness versus limitless love.

Jonah wanted to boil a broth of unbrotherly hate to the savage satisfaction of his own selfish soul and see the Ninevites damned. God had to work miracles to change him, and the greatest of all was the change of his unlimited littleness into the limitless love of JHWH.

JHWH added concerning Nineveh this heart-searching, heartbreaking word, "wherein are more than sixscore thousand persons that cannot discern between their right hand and their left hand." Sixscore thousand are one hundred and twenty thousand. Those that know not the difference between their right and their left hand are babies. A hundred and twenty thousand babies! Will you condemn them to die for the sins of their fathers and mothers? Will you fume and fuss about your gourds while you leave them to their fate?

Who dares to tell God who can be saved and who cannot? We are told that Kagawa of Japan is the child of a *geisha* woman. The love that sent missionaries to Japan found Kagawa, and Kagawa's ministry now glorifies the missionary enterprise.

"Red and yellow, black and white,
All are precious in his sight,
All the little children of the world."

Love for them determines our attitude toward the difficulties. One day an elderly gentleman stood watching a group of children playing tag. One small girl carried a baby brother on her back. Finally breathless, she paused for rest beside this man. Touched with fatherly solicitude, he said to her, "He is too heavy for you, my dear." "Oh, no sir," she answered, "he is my brother!"

JHWH added, "and much cattle." Even prevention of cruelty to animals is a worthy aim of the limitless love of God.

Conclusion

"Whenever shallow humor prompts people to hold the Old Testament up to ridicule, Balaam's ass and Jonah's whale infallibly take precedence." These were the words of Carl Heinrich Cornill, one-time professor of Old Testament history in the University of Königsberg, Germany. Surely he was not one to be accused of credulity or unwarranted sentiment. Yet, he challenged such shallow humor with the following confession of faith and feeling: "I have read the book of Jonah at least a hundred times, and I will publicly avow, for I am not ashamed of my weakness, that I cannot even now take up this marvelous book, nay, nor even speak of it, without tears rising to my eyes, and my heart beating higher. This apparently trivial book is one of the deepest and grandest that was ever written, and I should like to say to every one who approaches it, 'Take off thy shoes for the place whereon thou standest is holy ground.' In this book Israelitic prophecy quits the scene of battle as victor, and as victor in its severest struggle—that against self."

In hearty accord with these words, let us add that they are true because Jonah went home to teach his own people their responsibility for missions. Accordingly, he abides in the heart of our Bible, asking every one of us, "Gourds or Souls?"

INTRODUCTION TO AMOS

Parallel Reading

Robertson, James, "Amos," in *ISBE*.
Taylor, J., "Amos," in *HDB*.
Driver, S. R., *LOT*, chap. VI, sec. 3.
Kirkpatrick, A. F., *Doctrines of the Prophets*, chap. IV.

Name

The name Amos as indicated in 1:1, is that of the author. It means "Burdensome" or "Burden-bearer."

Date and Authorship

The authorship of the prophet Amos and his time are also indicated in 1:1. As the reigns of Uzziah and Jeroboam were both long and over-lapped for many years, their reigns alone do not fix the date very pointedly. However, remembering Jonah's prophecy of prosperity for Jeroboam, we place Amos' prophecy of approaching doom in Amos 7:9 near the end of Jeroboam's reign, about 760 B.C.

Purpose and Method

The purpose that rules all the way through is to interpret JHWH's judgment of Israel. Israel is of course the Ten Tribes of the Northern Kingdom, not Israel as synonymous with Jacob. The method is that of prophetic oratory, adroitly arranged to rise gradually and repeatedly to periodic emphasis on the judgment of Israel.

[115]

OUTLINE

JHWH's Judgment of Israel, the Ten Tribes

Title: 1:1

Text: 1:2. Cf. Joel 3:16.

I

Nations Will Be Punished. 1:3 to 2:5

1. Syria, for cruelty in war, by war and
   captivity 1:3-5
2. Philistia, for slave-trading, by war and
   complete destruction 1:6-8
2. Tyre, for slave-trading, by war 1:9-10
4. Edom, for unbrotherly hatred, by
   war 1:11-12
5. Ammon, for savage cruelty, by war and
   captivity of rulers 1:13-15
6. Moab, for sacrilege, by war and destruction of rulers 2:1-3
7. Judah, for rejection of the law of JHWH,
   by war 2:4-5

II

Children of Israel Will Be Terribly Punished.
2:6 to 4:13

1. Because they have become morally corrupt as the Amorites were 2:6-16
2. Because of abuse of God's favor 3:1-8
3. Because of oppressions and violence 3:9-12
4. Because of the altars of Bethel 3:13-15
5. Because of corrupt women 4:1-3

III

House of Israel Will Be Destroyed by Captivity. 5:1 to 6:14

IV

Chastisement of Israel Will Lead to Restoration Under the Davidic Line. 7:1 to 9:15

5. Vision of the summer fruit: JHWH will
bring the nation of Israel to an end 8:1-14

6. Vision of the destroyed altar: JHWH
will destroy the sinners in Israel as any
other sinners 9:1-10

7. Vision of the restoration: JHWH will
raise up the tabernacle of David over all
Israel in permanent possession of the
promised land 9:11-15

TEXTUAL NOTES

Indications of Outline

In chapters 1-2 it is obvious that a list of nations
shapes the message. There are seven of these before Israel is addresed, forming a natural unit according to Hebrew thinking. Chapters 3-4 continue
the message to Israel started in 2:6-16. However,
Israel is addressed in 3:1 as "children of Israel," so
that it is the people rather than the government.
3:13 does speak of "the house of Jacob," but it is
referred to rather than addressed. To the end of
chapter 4 it is the people that are the center of
thought. In 5:1 "the house of Israel," the reigning
line, is addressed, becomes the subject, and remains
so through chapter 6. In chapters 7-9 Jacob, the
whole of the Israelitish people, including those of
both kingdoms, becomes the subject. Definite distinctions are made in the results of JHWH's judgment in each of these cases. Thus, these facts indicate the main developments of thought.

1:2 The first part of this verse is the same as the first part of Joel 3:16. It is used by Amos like a text. Upon the theory of Joel's early date as we hold it, this use of the text from his prophecy is a fine example of the characteristic trait of prophecy which leads a prophet to build upon the work of predecessors. Likewise, it becomes a fine example for preachers of today.

1:3,6,9,11,13; 2:1,4,6. The expression, "For three transgressions . . . , yea, for four," doubtless has a "manifold significance," as F. W. Farrar points out. Going on, he comes to the heart of the matter in these words, "It implies that the wickedness which called down the judgment was growing and increasing from year to year." We may add that the number three probably indicated fulness and four an overflow. In connection with the case of Israel in 2:6, we may also add a fact arising out of study of Kings. Jeroboam II, king of Israel at the time of this prophecy, represented the house of Jehu. The house of Jehu was the fourth to reign over Israel. Those of Jeroboam the son of Nebat, of Baasha, and of Ahab had been judged already. Yet another point may appear in this word to Jehu, "Thy sons to the fourth generation shall sit on the throne of Israel." (2 Kings 10:30; 15:12) Jeroboam II was the third generation after Jehu. His son was to be fourth and last. Amos' burning phrase could refer to the house of Jehu as the fourth reigning line to be condemned and to the son of Jeroboam as the fourth and last of his house to sit on the throne.

1:4,7,10,12,14; 2:2,5. "A fire" symbolized the conflagration and destruction of invasion and war, specifically represented by the approaching Assyrian conquests. It was used by Amos in the first seven cases he dealt with to present summarily his picture of their judgment. The case of Israel being his main topic, he dealt with it in detail.

2:11,16; 3:10,13,15; 4:3,5-6,8-11; 6:8, 14; 8:3, 9,11; 9:7-8,12,13. "Saith Jehovah," in these twenty-one instances represents a Hebrew word with peculiarly important force. It marks, with greater power than any other word in the language, the fact that the accompanying prophecy is the very word of JHWH. There are various other ordinary words used to state this fact. These may be observed at many other places in Amos, as in 1:3,6,9,11,13; 2:1, 4,6. This one is special. It may be impossible to grasp this word fully with our words. Probably the most distinctive rendering is, This is the express utterance of JHWH.

Prophets use this word to emphasize their high points. Thus David used it with Psalm 110, Joel once, Hosea four times, others often. Amos used it more perhaps in proportion to volume of the message than any other prophet. Nevertheless, he used it with consummate skill, each time driving home vital points in his message.

All these vital points in Amos, marked by this expression, deal with the judgment of Israel. Moreover, the concentration of them in certain parts of the message marks the final word concerning each phase of Israel's judgment.

3:12. "Two legs, or a piece of an ear," tells with startling reality the condition in which judgment will leave the children of Israel. It implies the preservation of a remnant, but a maimed and miserable remnant.

4:1. "Kine of Bashan," or "Cows of Bashan," refers to the women of Samaria. What blasting sarcasm!

4:4-5. This is ironical and satirical. A true prophet's invitation to Bethel could not be otherwise than ironical. Invitation to transgress and to offer sacrifice "of that which is leavened" runs into satire. The statement, "for it pleases you," touches the core of all this corruption plainly and directly. All this tells Israel to go ahead and transgress, in as much as that is what she has chosen to do, and then take the consequences.

4:12. "Prepare to meet thy God," is not a call to repentance. In accord with what precedes, it is a warning of judgment.

5:1. "Lamentation" is a dirge, a funeral song for "the house of Israel."

5:2. "She shall no more rise," states with simple finality the permanence of the fall of Israel's government.

5:3. Again the remnant is indicated, but it will be insufficient to raise up the kingdom of Israel.

7:1-3. The reference to Jacob in 7:2 shows that the message has turned to the whole of Israel after finishing with the children of Israel, or the Ten Tribes, and with the house of Israel. It appears from 3:13 that the Ten Tribes had developed the habit of emphasizing their relation to the whole by calling the house of Israel the house of Jacob. Since Amos has prophesied permanent destruction of that house and also the preservation of a remnant of the children of Israel, the question naturally arises, What will be the connection in the days to come between the remnant and Jacob, Israel as a whole? The series of seven visions beginning here deals with this question and indicates final restoration under "the tabernacle of David," the Davidic line.

7:1-3. The "latter growth" of Jacob is the subject of this passage. The Lord's answer in 7:3 is that the threat of extermination will be merely a threat.

7:4-6. The second vision concerns "the land." "The land" should be rendered "the portion." (Cf. footnote of *ASV*.) The ordinary word for land is not used but that which describes the Promised Land as the land apportioned to Israel by JHWH. Thus the question is, Will the coming judgment revoke the promise concerning the land of Israel? The answer is No! The first of invasion devours the deep and threatens the land, but there it is stopped.

7:7-9. The plumb line is a symbol of righteousness. JHWH's righteousness requires the judgment of Israel's people and rulers as already pictured.

This will go forward as a part of the fulfilment of the promises concerning Jacob.

7:10-17. The occasion for the vision concerning Amaziah is an historical incident. The description of it by many commentators as an historical interlude need not lead us to view it as a break in the continuity of Amos' message. It is merely the occasion for another vision directly in line with the preceding and the succeeding. The terrible punishment of Amaziah's wife may be considered as bringing out the character already in her, not an imposition of a character contrary to her real self. Thus it is with all of idolatrous Israel, even priests, their wives, and their children. Righteousness on God's part requires this, and his prophets should be consistently interpreted as thinking within the sphere of his ethical monotheism.

8:1-14. The summer fruit marks the end of the season for fruit. Therefore, "the end is come," says that the predicted judgment is at hand.

9:1-10. Destruction of the altar symbolized removal of the sanctuary as a place of escape from judgment. No horns of the altar left to lay hold upon so as to stay the avenger of blood! So it is, "though they dig into Sheol" or "though they climb up to heaven," judgment will overtake them. No escape! Like all other sinners!

9:11-15. 9:11 pictures restoration under the Davidic line. 9:14 pictures the inclusion of all Israel. 9:15 declares the permanent possession of the Promised Land.

CRITICAL PROBLEMS

VI

Is Amos 9:8b-15 the Work of the Prophet Amos?

Because of widespread claims of composite authorship and corrupted texts in the prophets, it is worth-while for all Old Testament students to examine with care a conspicious example like Amos 9:8b-15. Some difficulties in the texts must be admitted, some accepted as insoluble perhaps, but it is good to realize that many of the claims need not disturb us at all.

C. H. Cornill speaks of the concluding part of Amos as a "reconciliatory conclusion . . . appended to the Book of Amos, which contains little of his ideas, and is at variance in all points with his doctrines."[1]

T. H. Robinson says, "It would seem that the more hopeful tone of 9:8b-15 is due to a compiler who could not bear the thought of the final destruction of his people."[2]

Alexander Gordon says, "The lovely picture of Israel's restoration (9:8b-15) is regarded by almost all recent scholars as an addition to the authentic words of Amos, couched in the ideas and language of later prophecy, and presupposing the actual fall of the kingdom of Judah (v. 11)."[3] He goes so far as to say below that it contradicts his former messages.

---

[1]Cornill, C. H., *Prophets of Israel*, p. 47.
[2]Robinson, T. H., *Prophecy and the Prophets*, p. 71.
[3]Gordon, Alexander, *Prophets of the Old Testament*, p. 58, note 2.

F. W. Farrar, on the other hand, says, "It is not improbable that the Messianic epilogue was an afterthought of hope and consolation, not delivered to the idolaters of Bethel and Samaria, but addressed in writing to all who waited for the consolation of Israel."[4]

J. R. Sampey agrees with Farrar in these words: "Whether or not, the encouraging words concerning the preservation of a faithful remnant in Israel were spoken to audiences in northern Israel, it seems to the present writer that they are genuine words of Amos. When he returned to Judah and wrote out his prophecies, these words of promise and hope formed a fitting conclusion to his bitter denunciation of Israel's sins."[5]

The foregoing textual notes contain much evidence bearing on this question. They point to a definite outline of thought which is most fittingly concluded with this conclusion as it stands. The first two of the seven visions in chapters 7-9 open the way for this concluding one, and the thought of the group is not complete without the last.

THEOLOGICAL STUDIES
VIII
Distinctive Contributions of Amos

Distinctive contributions of Amos are seen as follows:

1. Everlasting condemnation of "the house of Israel." As Kings records, prophets preceding

[4]Farrar, F. W., *The Minor Prophets*, p. 47.
[5]Sampey, J. R., "Notes on Amos" in *Review and Expositor*, Vol. XXX, for July, 1933.

Amos condemned one family of kings after another. Amos made the term, "house of Israel," to cover all Israel's rulers, to condemn all, and to condemn them everlastingly.

2. Restoration of Israel under the Davidic line.

3. Points in the perfection of JHWH's justice.
    a. It mercifully delays, yet inevitably comes. (Cf. notes concerning the expression, "For three transgressions . . . yea, for four"; also 9:10.)
    b. All its reasons for condemnation have moral foundations. (Cf. Section I of the outline; also 7:7-9.)
    c. It demands more of those who know more. (Cf. 3:2.)
    d. It eternally damns hypocrites. (Cf. Section III of outline.)
    e. There is no escape from it. (Cf. Section IV-6 of outline.)
    f. There is no respect of persons in it. (Cf. 9:7-10.)
    g. There is a purifying purpose controlling it. (9:7-10.)

4. Demand for righteousness in JHWH's people.

This is present in the messages of all true prophets, but receives a peculiarly clear and powerful emphasis in all parts of Amos. Its finest statement comes in 5:24, "But let justice roll down as waters, and righteousness as a mighty stream."

INTRODUCTION TO HOSEA

Parallel Reading

Robertson, James, "Hosea," in *ISBE*.

Davidson, A. B., "Hosea," in *HDB*.

Driver, S. R., *LOT*, chap. VI, sec. 1.

Kirkpatrick, A. F., *Doctrine of the Prophets*, chap. V.

Name

The name Hosea, as indicated in 1:1, is that of the author. It means Deliverance or Salvation.

Date and Authorship

The authorship of the prophet Hosea and his time are also indicated by 1:1. The reigns of the kings mentioned, counting from the end of Uzziah's to the beginning of Hezekiah's, make his ministry at the least to cover the period 735-727 B.C. 1:4 probably carries the beginning back into the reign of Jeroboam II. The troubled conditions reflected in chapters 4-14 indicate continuance toward the end of the Northern Kingdom in 722 B.C. Thus we approximate the period 750-725 B.C. for Hosea's ministry.

Purpose and Method

Chapters 1-3 appear to have a historical background, but the purpose controlling its use is to prophesy concerning JHWH's future redemption of Israel. Chapters 4-14 are so broken in thought and arrangement as to defy detailed outlining, yet as a whole are just as plainly prophetic as is the first part concerning Israel's sore punishment for sin and

[127]

restoration by faith. They appear as the passionate outpourings of a broken heart that allows its overwhelming feelings to flow without effort or desire to disguise the disorder caused by their flood-tide of grief. Yet, over the receding storm clouds there rises a rainbow of hope.

OUTLINE

JHWH's Redeeming Love
Title: 1:1

I

Lessons Concerning JHWH's Love

Learned in the School of Experience.
Chapters 1-3

Int. JHWH leads his prophet to love one of the idolatrous people about him 1:2

1. The lesson through the first child, Jezreel ..1:3-5 No continued mercy for those guilty of the blood of Jezreel.

2. The lesson through the second child, Loruhamah ....1:6-7 No mercy forever for the House of Israel, but there will be mercy for the House of Judah.

3. The lesson through the third child, Loammi ....1:8-9 No mercy for the present people of Israel.

4. The lesson through the unfaithful wife ....1:10 to 3:5

(1) JHWH's example ....1:10 to 2:23
    Int. Assurance of a future, full,
    and faithful Israel ....1:10 to 2:1
    a. JHWH's chastening love will
    force Israel to recognize her
    folly 2:2-13
    b. JHWH's redeeming love will re-
    new and perpetuate Israel's love
    for him 2:14-20
    c. JHWH's perfecting love will
    abundantly bless Israel in Jez-
    reel 2:21-23
(2) The prophet's emulation 3:1-5
    Int. Directed by JHWH 3:1a
    a. He ransoms the unfaithful wife
    from slavery 3:1b-2
    b. He isolates her and woos her
    again in hope of such reunion as
    JHWH's love shall accomplish
    with Israel 3:3-5

II

Messages Concerning JHWH's Love

Spoken to an Unfaithful People. Chapters 4-14

1. No mercy now for the children of Israel
  because they are corrupt ....Chapter 4
2. No mercy for the priests and princes
  because they lead the people into corruption ....Chapters 5-7
3. No preservation for the worship of Israel
  because it is false ....Chapters 8-10

4. Despite Israel's stubbornness, JHWH's love will lead to repentance and healing ....Chapters 11-14

CRITICAL PROBLEMS

VII

Marriage of Hosea

Three main interpretations have arisen. These are as follows:

Allegorical Interpretation

Interpretation of the marriage as an allegory was advocated by John Calvin. Objection to marriage with an unchaste woman was made on moral grounds. "Wife of whoredom," in 1:2 was interpreted as a prostitute. Stress was laid on the agreement that God would not lead his prophet into such a contemptible position as marriage with a prostitute would entail. The children were made parts of the parable, but the woman of chapter 3 was seemingly considered different from that one in chapters 1-2.

Literal View Holding the Wife Unchaste Before Marriage

Some interpret "wife of whoredom" as Calvin, yet consider the experience real. It is considered an exceptional case in which God led his prophet along strange paths in order to present a very unusual example.

Literal View Holding the Wife Unfaithful After Marriage

Others interpret "wife of whoredom" as describing one belonging to the idolatrous and spiritually adulterous people of Hosea's day, not actually unchaste before marriage, but having the licentious tendencies of idolatry latent in her character.

The third interpretation is favored by the following facts:

1. It alone relieves the moral difficulty. Even Calvin's view did not do that. The use of an adulterous marriage to illustrate JHWH's love for his people, even in allegory, involves serious moral difficulties.

2. It preserves the natural identification of the woman in chapter 3 with that one in chapters 1-2 as well as number two does. This is quite important in interpreting the purpose of the message as a whole.

3. It interprets "whoredom" in the light of its immediate context in 1:2a as "departing from Jehovah."

4. It is possible that further evidence is to be seen in the fact that 1:3 definitely indicates the first child as his child while 1:6 and 1:8 do not do the same concerning the others.

THEOLOGICAL STUDIES

IX

Victory of JHWH's Love

The messianic implications of Hosea 3:1-5 are worthy of our most careful consideration. At this point the stream of messianic prophecy breaks forth from the rocky mountain peaks of the Day of JHWH and proceeds to gladden all succeeding pictures of that day. Evidence of messianic ideas have been noted before. There was Joel's outpouring of the spirit, Jonah's teaching concerning JHWH's compassion on the heathen, and Amos' view of restoration under the tabernacle of David. These are prophecies of a personal Messiah. In Hosea, the idea of a personal Messiah, seen in the Pentateuch, Samuel, and Psalms, is brought into the center of the picture. After Hosea this personal Messiah becomes a key to the fulfilment of all prophecy, thus magnifying the influence of Hosea's word concerning him. Messianic prophecies before Hosea are like signs of water beneath the mountains. In Hosea they make a spring. Afterward they make a river, "the streams whereof make glad the city of God" (Psalm 46:4).

Hosea 3:1-5 appears to teach that JHWH's love will yet redeem Israel as a nation from sin and win her love through Messiah. Careful consideration of chapters 1-3 as a unit is necessary in order to see this teaching. It has wonderful encouragement in it when once grasped. That is why the identification of the unfaithful wife of chapters 1-2 with the wife of chapter 3 is so important.

The command of Hosea in 3:1 to follow the example of JHWH in dealing with his wife implies that what he did do, again wooing and winning her, was done according to that example of JHWH. That

example of JHWH, as described in 2:2-23, applies
largely to the future. Therefore, the experience of
the prophet becomes a parallel to the prophecy of
JHWH's future dealing with Israel. Even the steps
in the prophet's revival of his wife's love may be
taken as illustrations of the stages in JHWH's expected revival of Israel's love. Thus, the whole account is made a prophecy.

I

Method of the Victory

1. Willing to win
   This is in the atmosphere of this story.
2. Warning against sin
   2:2-3 and chap. 4-10 are full of illustrations.
3. Chastisement for sin
   Cf. 2:6-13; 3:4; 5:14-15; 7:12; 8:11-14; 9:17;
   13:9.
4. Redemption from the slavery of sin
   3:2 described the paying of the usual price of a
   slave in the market. Thus, the wife is pictured
   as having become a slave because of her sins and
   the husband as paying a redemption price. The
   redemption of the cross of Christ is foreshadowed.
5. Waiting for the response
   3:3 indicated the revival of the wife's first love
   was not expected immediately, but patiently,
   confidently, purposefully awaited. Consumma-
   tion is allowed to wait upon realization of what
   had been done for her, appreciation, faith, and
   love.

6. Wooing unto renewed affection, respect, and betrothal
   2:14-15a; 11:8-11 are examples of the persistent wooing that goes on.
7. Restoration as JHWH's own people
   2:21-23; 3:5; 14:4-8 describe the fruits of victory, the abundant blessings of complete restoration.

II

Manner of the Victory

1. Constraining
   3:4 shows all the punishment during the day of JHWH to be exercised as loving constraint leading Israel back to JHWH.   To be "without king, and without prince, and without sacrifice," would make the lack of fulfilment for prophecies concerning continuance of the Davidic line to be glaring in Israel's eyes.   To be "without pillar, and without ephod or teraphim" would tear away even the symbols of false worship and shut them up to trust in JHWH alone.

2. Charming
   3:5 shows that the seeking of JHWH is also a seeking of "David their king."   As the first David was long since dead, this is the second David. He is identified with JHWH in a unique sense in the predicted restoration of all Israel.   He is the earthly representative of JHWH.   In the restoration the attraction of JHWH is seen as identified with him rather than any of the old

symbols of worship. He becomes king, king of all Israel, the king of kings whose charm brings Israel back to JHWH.

3. Converting

The answer of 2:15b is to be made by Israel. It is to be an answer, a free response, not a forced result. The calling of JHWH "Ishi," "my husband," in 2:16, instead of "Baali," "my master," indicates a change of attitude caused by a new appreciation and respect. Thus the new covenant is "in righteousness, and in justice, and in lovingkindness, and in mercies . . . even . . . in faithfulness" (2:19-20). This is a crowning statement of the way of salvation according to the theology of ethical monotheism.

The seeking of JHWH predicted in 3:5 is voluntary.

"Take with you words, and return to Jehovah" in 14:2, indicates repentance, confession, and faith; in a word, this passage describes conversion.

III
Means of the Victory

As the love of the prophet for his wife was to be an emulation of the example of JHWH, so the love of JHWH is the means of this victory. It is pictured in detail as follows:

1. Love in spite of unfaithfulness. (Cf. 2 Tim. 2:13.)

As the wife was "beloved of her friend" (3:1), she was the unfaithful party. Though the husband might have considered himself free, his love made him refuse to give her up.

2. Love in spite of adultery
The addition of the words, "and an adulteress" (3:1), seems to make the first description, "beloved of a friend," to apply to attitude, and this one to the act. Yet, the husband remained faithful.

3. Love in spite of desertion
"Though they turn unto other gods" (3:1), describes more than isolated acts of unfaithfulness. This is open desertion. Yet, the husband is faithful.

4. Love in spite of prostitution
"And love cakes of raisins" (3:1), describes love for hire, or prostitution. (Cf. 2:12.) This is the lowest degradation of unfaithfulness, far deeper in vileness and further from hope than sudden, overwhelming, and hated moments of passion. It is the love of the husband and that alone that keeps the lamp of hope burning. That kind of love takes the initiative, never gives up, and proves itself mighty to save.
Thus Hosea becomes the prophet of redeeming love. His experience gives one of the deepest insights into JHWH's love for sinners to be found in the Old Testament.

INTRODUCTION TO MICAH

Parallel Reading

Orelli, C. von, "Micah," in *ISBE*.
Nowach, W., "Micah," in *HDB*.
Driver, S. R., *LOT,* chap. VI, sec. 6.
Kirkpatrick, A. F., *Doctrine of the Prophets,* chap.
VII.

Name

The name Micah, as shown in 1:1, is that of the
author. It means "Who Is Like JHWH?" 7:18
shows that the meaning of the name was emphasized
in the prophet's thinking and message.

Date and Authorship

The authorship of the prophet and his time are
also marked by 1:1. The omission of Uzziah from
the list of kings shows that Micah's ministry began
very shortly after that of Isaiah, whose call came in
the year that Uzziah died. The absence of any mention of Samaria or reference to the Northern Kingdom after chapter 1 indicates that his ministry continued after 721 B.C. Lack of any word reflecting the
reforms of Hezekiah make us suppose it did not continue far into the day of his best work. As outside
limits we can set 735 and 700 B.C., but the period
was probably not so long. 1:1 also tells us the
prophet was a Morashtite, and his native village is
probably to be identified with Moresheth-gath of
1:14, which lay about seventeen miles from Jerusalem in the foothills of the Judean mountains over-
looking the territory of Gath in the Philistine plain.
The actual view from Moresheth-gath was doubtless

the background for the prophetical picture of invasion given in 1:8-16.

Purpose and Method

As Orelli observes concerning Micah, "he loved antitheses,"[1] and the appearance of this peculiarity with others throughout the book strengthens the argument that all of it was the work of Micah. However, even Orelli gives no evidence that he recognized a certain remarkable set of antitheses in the book. Two or three he mentioned but to the whole group and its remarkable arrangement he does not refer. Yet, this set of antitheses gives to the book a splendid outline and implements its purpose with tremendous force. In this general outline it appears clearly.

(Title: 1:1)

I Captivity is certain ....1:2 to 2:11
II Restoration from captivity is also
     certain 2:12-13
III Captivity is coming because of moral
     corruption 3:1-12
IV But Zion shall be restored to moral
     pre-eminence in the latter days.....4:1-8
V Captivity is coming because of lack
     of leadership ....4:9 to 5:1
VI But Israel shall be restored by
     Messiah 5:2-15
VII Captivity is coming because of faith-
     lessness ....6:1 to 7:6

[1]Orelli, C. von, "Micah," in *ISBE*, p. 2046.

VIII But Israel shall be restored through
          faith 7:7-20

The abrupt, striking, and purposeful turn of thought
in each case appears in a careful observation of the
text. In points IV, VI, and VIII, the "but" is taken
from the text. The co-ordination of the whole is the
strongest evidence of its conscious arrangement by
the prophet. It gives logical co-ordination to the
whole and to the details.

The purpose thus appears to be the announcement of the certainty of Judah's captivity and restoration. Isaiah and Micah use these two messages
together to explain each other, and to interpret the
whole future of Judah. It is impossible to say who
precedes the other in this or that point, but they
proceed harmoniously to fill out an exceedingly important sketch of future things, some of them yet
future to us. Obadiah, Joel, and Jonah implied
these things, but in very general ways. Amos and
Hosea prophesied directly concerning the Ten Tribes
and warned Judah. Now Isaiah and Micah come to
direct interpretation of Judah's destiny. It is a difficult task to interpret the casting off of Judah, for
her destiny includes that of the Davidic line. Their
purpose, however, includes the facing of this very
difficulty. Doing so faithfully, fearlessly, prayer-
fully, there come to them great visions of Messiah
and his reign that furnish the solution.

DETAILED OUTLINE

Certainty of Judah's Captivity and Restoration
Title: 1:1

I

Captivity is Certain. 1:2 to 2:11

1. JHWH's testimony condemns the people..1:2-7
2. The prophet bewails their fate..........1:8-16
3. Moral corruption necessitates such a fate.2:1-11

II

Restoration from Captivity is Likewise Certain.
2:12-13

III

Captivity is Coming Because of Moral Corruption.
3:1-12

1. The corruption of rulers.................3:1-4
2. The corruption of priests...............3:5-8
3. Hypocrisy is added to evil deeds.........3:9-12

IV

But Zion Will Be Restored to Moral Pre-eminence
in the Latter Days. 4:1-8

1. Zion will become a permanent medium
   of universal instruction and peace........4:1-5
2. The afflicted remnant of Israel will be
   made a permanent and God-directed
   kingdom in Zion 4:6-8

V

Captivity is Coming Because of Lack of
Leadership. 4:9 to 5:1

VI

But Israel Will Be Restored by Messiah. 5:2-15
Key: "To be a ruler in Israel." (5:2)

1. One born in Bethlehem..................5:2a
2. One going forth from everlasting..........5:2b
3. One who will restore and shepherd his brethren "in the strength of Jehovah".....5:3-4
4. One who will establish peace with the nations 5:5-6
5. One who will make "the remnant of Jacob" a supernatural influence among the nations 5:7-9
6. One who will remove militarism from his people 5:10-11
7. One who will remove idolatry from his people 5:12-15

VII

Captivity Is Coming Because of Faithlessness.
6:1 to 7:6

Int. JHWH demands an answer to his suit....6:1-2
1. The hearing 6:3-8
   (1) JHWH's question: Has he given any occasion for Israel's rejection of him? 6:3-5
   (2) Israel's reply: Can JHWH not be be satisfied with her lavish gifts..6:6-7
   (3) JHWH's answer: Nothing more required than "to do justly, to love kindness, and to walk humbly with God": JHWH desires their life, love, and trust 6:8

VIII

TEXTUAL NOTES

1:7. Critics have often claimed that this verse does not fit as a part of the work of Micah. Their arguments, however, seem odd, because they claim

that it lacks the force of the preceding verses. They
speak of it as though the punches of a champion
had suddenly become powderpuff pitter-patter. They
argue much about the meaning of the word translated "hires." A typical attitude appears in Well-
hausen's suggestion that a word similar in spelling
be substituted for the original which would make
the verse refer to idolatrous images.

Comparison with Hosea's use of the word "hire"
in Hosea 2:12; 8:10; 9:1 indicates that prophets
of this time used the word to describe what the
people thought to be the advantages or gain of idol
worship, but what JHWH called evidence of spiritual
harlotry. Comparison with Deuteronomy 23:18
shows that such gain was an abomination in
JHWH's eyes, and any offering drawn from such
sources absolutely unacceptable. Thus Micah was
telling Judah that her life had become an abomination and that JHWH would absolutely refuse to accept any sort of propitiation intended to save her
from captivity. In this light, we see that more
terrific and terrible words could not be found in all
the language of the Israelites.

It is in view of this awful picture that the lamentation or dirge of 1:8-16 is immediately begun. The
details of moral condemnation in 2:1-11 and 3:1-12
are simply enlargements of 1:7. No wonder that
these lead to the cry in 3:12, "Therefore shall Zion
for your sake be plowed as a field"! With such
peculiarly vivid power of language, Micah drove

home the certainty of captivity. 4:9 to 5:1 and 6:1 to 7:6 are other explanations of the same word.

2:12-13. The abrupt change of thought in these verses is of course obvious. Critics, prone to look for corrupted texts, have taken this as evidence of confusion. As the first of a series of purposeful antitheses, the passage gives no substantial ground for such criticism. Moreover the language is highly wrought and full of evidence that the author knew he was saying a very unusual thing. The language is so unusual as to be out of place without a setting like the antithesis we have noted to give provocation. These unusual points are not all clear in the English text, but cannot be overlooked in the Hebrew. They are:

(1) The verb "assemble" is given the strongest emphasis possible in the language for a verb. It might well be given a triple underscore in our words. We may take the use of "will" with it in the first person as carrying the fullest measure of determination, and remember at the same time that it is God who says it.

(2) The verb "gather" is emphasized in the same way.

(3) The description of the object of assemble and gather as a "remnant" presupposes exactly such events as are described in 1:2 to 2:11.

(4) The statement in 2:13, "The breaker is gone up before them," likewise presupposes captivity and the need for a breaker of bonds.

(5) The identification of the deliverer with JHWH presupposes a situation calling for a deliverance by no less a majesty than JHWH.

If this prediction of restoration stood alone, or this single antithesis alone, attacks upon its authenticity would have much greater chance to win a hearing.   But this brief picture of restoration is merely a miniature of what we find in 4:1-8, 5:2-15, and 7:7-20.   Moreover, each enlargement stands in similar pointed contrast with pictures of the coming captivity.

CRITICAL PROBLEMS

VIII

Interpolations in Amos, Hosea, and Micah

The texts of Amos, Hosea, and Micah are frequently attacked by charges of interpolation.   Such charges ought to be faced with an open mind and studied patiently.

The arguments touching these matters, which have been presented, have all led to refutation of such charges at important points.   It is not the author's intention, however, to deny the need for painstaking textual criticism, or to create an impression that every such charge has no foundation.   Trust that criticism has not and will not prove that our texts have been so altered by time and mishap as to be untrustworthy is thought to be warranted. Yet, it is admitted that some changes have crept in. Capable and faithful scholarship should be able to bridge the gaps by simply building in line with the highway of revelation. It ought to be able to do so without causing fear on the part of those who travel that highway that the work will prevent the safe arrival of some. Let those who discuss the gaps or those who bridge them be sure they know the line of the highway behind and before. The reason why more attention is not given to the unsolved difficulties is a conviction that they affect the whole message only slightly, in no essential sense altering its teaching. We turn aside to these problems occasionally to deal with matters which threaten the teaching, but we can do only a little of such work in a general survey. The teaching is our main concern.

Clear but brief presentation of critical charges will be found in Alexander Gordon's *Old Testament Prophets*. Treatment of the several books in *ICC* gives them in detail. James Robertson in *The Early Religion* of Israel gives grounds for refutation of many.

THEOLOGICAL STUDIES

X

Messiah as the God-man

Micah's great picture of Messiah is found in 5:2-15. Details are given in section VI of the outline. The points of supreme importance are the first two.

The prediction of birth in Bethlehem is the one widely known. It sees this future representative of the Davidic line making a new start from David's birthplace rather than the place of his throne, Jerusalem. This implies humiliations brought about by the judgment of Judah, and maybe origin from another Davidic line than that of Solomon. It parallels the message in Isaiah 11:1-10, picturing "a shoot out of the stock of Jesse, and a branch out of his roots."

The characterization of Messiah as one "whose goings forth are from of old, from everlasting" is not usually recognized for its full worth, but it has a worth beyond all expectation. The two together make this passage a parallel to Isaiah's prophecy of Immanuel in Isaiah 7:10-17. "Goings forth" are earthly activities, as seen in Job 34:21, Psalm 40:2, and Proverbs 20:24. "From of old," according to Psalm 44:1, means from the time of the fathers or patriarchs; according to Psalm 68:33, from the time the heavens were created; according to Psalm 93:2, from the establishment of JHWH's throne. Remembering that this ruler not merely existed at such olden time but continues "from of old," so as to be born in some later time, we see a wondrous one. He is like unto the Angel of JHWH, whose goings forth have been noted from the time of Abraham to that of Elijah. He is like unto the Personified Wisdom of Proverbs 8:22-31, who was with God at the creation. He is like unto JHWH himself in his everlasting reign. No wonder that the phrase, "from everlasting," was added by Micah! This wondrous one is nothing less than the God-man.

It is impossible to tell whether the pictures of Isaiah or Micah precede. Maybe each of these two great prophets was an inspiration to the other. We must think of them and their pictures as contemporaries.

XI

Emphasis on Faith

Sections VII and VIII place a great emphasis on faith. They need to be studied together to appreciate this emphasis. The suit in 6:1 to 7:6 is a trial in which Israel is found guilty of faithlessness. This makes the background for the cry of 7:7, "But as for me, I will look unto Jehovah, I will wait for the God of my salvation: my God will hear me." The picture of restoration is built upon this confession of faith. One lone soul that will trust is sufficient to evoke JHWH's assurance that he will yet save all Israel. As with Moses when Israel made the Golden Calf at Sinai, so now JHWH assures his prophet that by his faith Israel will be saved.

The much beloved statement in 6:8, "what doth Jehovah require of thee, but to do justly, and to love kindness, and to walk humbly with thy God," gives its supreme emphasis to faith. "To do justly" requires righteous living or deeds. "To love kindness" requires a right heart or motive. Deeds become the fruit and love the root. "To walk humbly" requires the forsaking of pride and self-will. Therefore, that which is the other side of the same thing, faith or trust in JHWH, becomes the ground from which love draws the sustenance of life eternal.

INTRODUCTION TO ISAIAH

Parallel Reading

Robinson. G. L.. "Isaiah," in *ISBE*.

Smith, G. A., "Isaiah," in *HDB*.

Driver, S. R., *LOT*, chap. III.

Kirkpatrick, A. F., *Doctrine of the Prophets*, chaps. VI, XIII, XVI.

Name

The name Isaiah, as indicated in 1:1, is that of the author. It means JHWH Saves or JHWH Is Salvation. The name symbolizes the message.

Date and Authorship

There is much dispute as to whether or not Isaiah, the son of Amoz, wrote all of the book. His name is unquestionably linked with parts of it by titles. These are found in 1:1; 2:1; 13:1. There are also references to him in 7:3; 20:2-3, and ten times in the historical section, chapters 36-39. No intimation is given by the book itself that there were other contributions to its prophetic messages. Jewish and Christian students till near the beginning of the nineteenth century accepted him as the author of the whole. A great number of modern Old Testament scholars have concluded that Isaiah did not write all. Various sections, especially chapters 40-66, are attributed by them to anonymous authors. They claim that the book gives no indication as to who wrote these sections.

Opinions as to date vary with opinions as to authorship. The ministry of Isaiah, the son of Amoz, began in Jerusalem in the year that Uzziah

died, as shown in chapter 6. That was about 740 B.C.
It continued through the reign of Hezekiah till sometime after 698 B.C. He is thought by many to have
been a native of Jerusalem and of princely lineage.
Other supposed authors are put near the end of the
captivity in 535 B.C. or later.

It appears impossible to prove conclusively that
there was only one Isaiah or more than one.   In-
ternal evidence is the only kind we have, and that
seems insufficient to close the argument.

We cannot afford, however, to dismiss this question of authorship as unimportant.   Careful examination of the effects of one's decision as to authorship upon one's appraisal of the teachings of the
book should surely awaken students to the vital importance of the decision.   Theoretically, it is easy to
say that it does not matter.   Practically, the effect
is tremendous.   Commentators' interpretations of
the teaching concerning Israel's destiny, concerning
Messiah's work and person, and concerning the plan
of salvation seem to vary with their decisions on this
point.   While the student's decision is pending and
he weighs the evidence for himself, let him by all
means determine to view the book as a unit and see
the importance of each part.   If uncertainty as to
authorship leads to doubt concerning the integrity
of the book as a whole, then one allows his own questions to bring the teachings of one of the greatest
books in the Bible into partial eclipse.

Method and Purpose

The method of Isaiah first impresses one with its
literary artistry.   There is much more in it than the

beauty of *belles-lettres,* but it is the fine writing that captures attention first of all.

The book is recognized as the literary masterpiece of all Hebrew writing. Vocabulary and style are superbly varied, beautiful, and meaningful. More words are used than in Jeremiah, Ezekiel, or all the Psalms. As for style, we find prose, poetry, oratory, song, homily, interrogation, dialogue, story, antithesis, alliteration, irony, sarcasm, satire, epigram, metaphor, hyperbole, play on words, and so on. Almost every means of embellishing literary style is used.

The interpreter of Isaiah, however, needs to go far beyond mere admiration of literary gems. It is easy to wander around, entranced by one beautiful word picture after another, until hopelessly lost mentally amid the intricacy and profusion of the thought. One needs to realize that Isaiah's word-jewels are like diamonds in a fine watch, set as bearings on which a message pivots and revolves. Then a disciplined study of them is necessary, a study as rigid in its logic as that which guided the author when he created them.

Diligence and discernment will soon see that the method of Isaiah is logical, homiletical, messianic, and philosophical, as well as literary.

The logic becomes impressive when we line up the points. It is not cast in the form of syllogisms. Each point is so neatly nestled in literary decoration that the harsh impression of argument is almost entirely avoided. Nevertheless, when we brush aside the frills for the sake of study and sight along the line of sharply defined points, we observe a compelling logic that brings hitherto unseen truths into view as a telescope does a star. Logic evidently put the message of chapter 1 at the beginning. It describes events later than some described in succeeding chapters; so it must have been placed according to a logical plan rather than the time described. Likewise, all the messages of chapters 2-12 manifest a logical sequence. To facilitate study of this sequence, double titles for each message have been arranged in the outline that follows. The first title in each case is the popular one, drawn from the obvious ideas in the prophet's introduction. The second title in each case is the logical one, drawn from the prophet's conclusion or message as a whole. Likewise, throughout the book, a logical order appears. Let the student line up the points of this logical order with care, if he would see the teaching of the book.

Homiletics appears in the way the prophet's logic shuts up every soul unto condemnation for sin and then points out the way unto salvation. All his methods are bent with consummate skill to serve the purposes of a preacher and a prophet. This sermonic art creates classic examples in the introductions to messages. The introductions not merely arrest attention but lead it to the heart of the message about sin or salvation that runs through all subsidiary points. Therefore, discrimination concerning the main point of an introduction will tell what is the subject of a message. In the same way, the appearance of a second introduction marks the end of the preceding message. An outstanding example of these introductions is the song at the beginning of chapter 5. Moreover, certain messages become introductions to groups of messages. Thus chapter 1 introduces all the messages concerning judgment, all of chapters 2-35; and chapter 40 introduces all the messages concerning comfort, all of chapters 41-66. This tells us that the book is a collection of prophetic sermons, written separately, from time to time over a long ministry, with a diversity of circumstances which often causes us to jump to the conclusion that they are not closely related. Nevertheless, this homiletical order also tells us that the collection is now arranged according to an order intended to make each message fit into a great general message.

Messianic solution of problems for which no other solution appears is another feature of Isaiah's method. Its logic, starting from Israel's history in chapter 1, with overwhelming evidence of Israel's tendency toward apostasy, leads to predictions of national doom. That same logic, starting from the promises of JHWH concerning the destiny of Israel, as in chapter 2, leads to faith in a glorious future. The reconciliation between the logic of the history and the logic of the promises becomes a question of supreme importance. Messiah furnishes this reconciliation. As other prophets before him, particularly Moses and Hosea, Isaiah sees that the only possible reconciliation will be the intervention of a divine being, able to break the seductive power of sin. More than all others, he describes the ways whereby Messiah will solve this problem that defies the power of mere man. The description of Immanuel in chapter 7 is a superlative illustration. He sees Immanuel as a sign given to test the faithlessness of Ahaz and condemn the reigning line of Israel from Solomon on down, yet to preserve at the same time the line of David through the virgin mother. All the way through, he makes such miraculous solutions to be the saving links, the "lap-links," of his logic. Apart from these solutions, we would condemn his prophecies concerning Israel's glorious future as wishful thinking and fanatical dreams. To understand his message, we must be sure to understand his conceptions of Messiah as the Davidic King, as the Suffering Servant, and as the Glorified One.

A philosophy of world history is built upon the logical developments already mentioned. The necessity for purging Israel of corrupting elements leads to visions of JHWH's use of other nations to punish her. In turn the treatment of Israel by other nations is seen as JHWH's means of determining whether or not they fear him. All history is a testing ground whereon JHWH destroys the unbelieving and saves believing remnants out of all nations. Messiah is seen as watching over all developments to promote his kingdom. He intervenes to preserve a remnant of Israel from annihilation, to bring back unto God remnants out of Israel and out of the nations, to use the Gentile remnants in restoring Israel to its own land, and to create new heavens and a new earth. Sketches of the new order, which becomes the goal of history, appear in 2:2-4 and chapter 12. The first comprehensive view appears in chapters 24-27. It is characterized by abstract terms and generalizations which fit it to be called a philosophy. In chapters 60-66, this new order is described again in terms of glory shared by elements out of all nations which come to worship JHWH. It is thoroughly spiritual and universal, and it gives a crowning scene to this philosophy of world history.

Three main purposes are served by all phases of Isaiah's method: (1) maintenance of faith in JHWH's final success in blessing Judah and Jerusalem; (2) revelation of Messiah as JHWH's supreme means of accomplishing all his work; (3) construction of a philosophy of world history with the universal, spiritual kingdom of God as its goal.

GENERAL OUTLINE OF ISAIAH
BOOK OF JUDGMENT
Int. Nature of Judgment...............Chap. 1
A. Judgment of Judah and Jerusalem..Chaps. 2-12
B. Judgment of the Nations..........Chaps. 13-23
C. Judgment of the World..........Chaps. 24-35

HISTORICAL ACCOUNTS Chaps. 36-39
BOOK OF COMFORT
Int. Certainty of Restoration............Chap. 40
A. Israel Returned ....Chaps. 41-48
B. Israel Saved ....Chaps. 49-59
C. Israel Glorified ....Chaps. 60-66

Notes Concerning Major Divisions

A distinction between the prophecies of chapters 1-35 and those of chapters 40-66 is implied by the placing of an historical section between them. Reasons for this distinction are made clear by the message of each section.

Primary bits of evidence indicating that chapters 1-35 deal with judgment appear in the following: (1) the introductory chapter deals with the nature of judgment; (2) the word concerning (literally against), found in the title of chapters 2-12, indicates a sentence of judgment; (3) the word "burden," so often used in chapters 13-23, seems to indicate the dreaded responsibility of pronouncing doom on nations; (4) the keynote of chapters 24-35, found in 24:1, is, "Jehovah maketh the earth empty."

Primary bits of evidence indicating that chapters 40-66 deal with comfort appear in the following: (1) 40:1 voices an appeal for the comfort of Israel which is answered by these chapters as a whole; (2) chapter 40 stresses the certainty of Israel's restoration as an introductory word; (3) chapters 41-48 picture return from Babylonian captivity as the first stage of this comfort; (4) chapters 49-59 picture salvation from sin as the second stage; and (5) chapters 60-66 picture the glory of restored leadership in the kingdom of God as the final stage.

DETAILED OUTLINE OF ISAIAH

BOOK OF JUDGMENT

Introduction: Nature of Judgment

(Title: 1:1)

A. Judgment of Judah and Jerusalem. Chaps. 2-12

(Title: 2:1)

I

Glory of the Latter Days

Prediction of Judgment Before Glory. Chaps. 2-4

II

The Song of the Unfruitful Vineyard
Parable of the Necessity for Judgment. Chap. 5

1. The failure of JHWH's blessing to insure
   fruitage 5:1-2
2. JHWH's determination to do the one
   thing that remains to be done to save his
   people, punish 5:3-7
3. Woes to follow 5:8-23
   (1) Upon land grabbers 5:8-10
   (2) Upon drunkards 5:11-17
   (3) Upon malicious and defiant sinners
       ....5:18-19
   (4) Upon the morally blind...........5:20
   (5) Upon those who trust self only...5:21
   (6) Upon those who corrupt justice.5:22-23
Con. A picture of the coming judgment....5:24-30
   (1) As terrible and prolonged......5:24-25
   (2) As inflicted by an invading army 5:26-30

III

Call of Isaiah

Revelation of Judgment Continued Until the
Land Be Desolate. Chap. 6

1. A vision of JHWH 6:1-4
2. Confession of sin 6:5
3. Assurance of cleansing 6:6-7
4. Offer to prophesy 6:8

IV

Sign of Immanuel: Test of Faith

Revelation of the Turning Point in Judgment.

Chap. 7

  He is the assurance of the perfection of
  the faithful

  He is the perfection of the assurance of
  the faithful

  He is the condemnation of the self-per-
  fection of the faithless

  He is the perfection of the condemnation
  of the faithless

V

Sign of Maher-shalal-hash-baz

Revelations of The Results of This Judgment. Chaps. 8-12

1. Invasion within a few years by King
   of Assyria 8:1-8
   (1) Spoiling of Damascus and Samaria 8:1-4
   (2) Overrunning of Judah also.......8:5-8
2. JHWH will become a sanctuary to those
   who trust in Him . . . (key verse:
   8:13-14a) 8:9-18
3. A night without a morning will come
   upon those who do not seek unto God ...
   (key verse: 8:20) 8:19-22
4. But a great light will shine upon Galilee
   in the latter time 9:1-7
   (1) Bringing honor 9:1, 2
   (2) Bringing increase of the nation 9:3
   (3) Bringing freedom 9:4
   (4) Bringing peace 9:5
   (5) Bringing gradual establishment of
       government and peace of Davidic
       Kingdom and everlasting mainte-
       nance of it in justice and righteous-
       ness 9:6, 7
5. The punishment of Samaria will continue on and on....................9:8 to 10:4
       (Key verses: 9:12b, 17b, 21b, 10:4b)
   (1) Repeated invasion 9:8-12
   (2) Cutting off of leaders..........9:13-17

   d. With victory over enemies
    . . . . .11:14
   e. By miraculous works of
    JHWH 11:15-16
  Con. The song of redeemed Israel. . . .12:1-6
   a. Thanks to JHWH for salva-
    tion 12:1-3
   b. Pleas unto Israel to make
    known the works of JHWH
    in all the earth 12:4-6

 B. Judgment of the Nations. Chaps. 13-23

I

The Burden of Babylon. 13:1 to 14:23
(Title: 13:1)

Int. JHWH calls the nations to battle. 13:2-5

1. All the world shall be punished. 13:6-16

2. The Medes shall destroy Babylon. 13:17-22

3. Jacob shall be restored. 14:1-27
 (1) Brought to their place by the na-
  tions 14:1-2
 (2) With exultation over fall of King of
  Babylon 14:3-20
 (3) Because JHWH will cut off name
  and remnant from Babylon forever
  . . . . .14:21-23
 (4) Because JHWH will make his pur-
  pose to break the Assyrian domination apply to all nations. 14:24-27

II

The Burden of Philistia
The remnant of Philistia shall be slain....14:28-32

III

The Burden of Moab. 15:1-16:14

1. Moab shall be destroyed by invasion....15:1-9
2. Fugitives shall take refuge with the
   House of David 16:1-5
3. This destruction shall be because of pride 16:6-12
4. Fulfilment shall come within three years 16:13-14

IV

The Burden of Damascus. 17:1-14

1. The glory of Damascus shall be made
   like that of Israel 17:1-3
2. The glory of Israel shall be made thin...17:4-11
3. Yet sudden destruction shall overtake
   the enemy 17:12-14

V

After judgment Ethiopians will bring
presents to JHWH....................18:1-7

VI

The Burden of Egypt. 19:1-25

1. JHWH's power will make Egypt fear
   Judah 19:1-17
2. JHWH shall be worshipped in Egypt..19:18-22
3. Egypt, Assyria, and Israel shall be
   united by the worship of JHWH and
   made a blessing in midst of the earth..19:23-25

VII

Dramatized Prediction that the King of
Assyria will take captives from Egypt
and Ethiopia 20:1-6

VIII

The Burden of the Wilderness of the Sea
Babylon will become a wilderness..........21:1-10

IX

The Burden of Dumah (Silence)
Times of darkness for Seir (Edom) will continue to come 21:11-12

X

The Burden of Arabia (Evening)
An evening time of waning glory will come
upon Arabia within a year............21:13-17

XI

The Burden of the Valley of Vision. 22:1-25
1. Jerusalem is condemned 22:1-14
   (1) For cowardice 22:1-4
   (2) For self-made plans of defense..22:5-11
   (3) For foolish carousal and bravado
       when called upon to repent....22:12-14
2. Shebna, the Treasurer, to be discharged
   and his place given to Eliakim.........22:15-25

XII

The Burden of Tyre: 23:1-18
Tyre shall be destroyed, but restored after
seventy years and made useful to
JHWH's people 23:1-18

C. Judgment of the World. Chaps. 24-35

I

JHWH's Righteousness will be revealed to All Men. 24:1-16a

II

Israel will be Made a Blessing to the World. 24:16b-33:24

(3) Purified . . . . 28:1 to 33:24

   a. Residue of Ephraim made to
      accept JHWH as a diadem
      of beauty 28:1-6

   b. Rulers in Jerusalem super-
      seded by a sure foundation,
      a precious corner stone 28:7-29

   c. Jerusalem delivered 29:1 to 31:9

     (a) Because she is to JHWH
         as Ariel, the altar hearth
         of God 29:1-8

     (b) To condemn the spirit-
         ually deaf and blind.29:9-24

     (c) Putting trust in Egypt
         to shame 30:1-26

     (d) The Assyrian being de-
         stroyed by JHWH's
         own hand . . . .30:27 to 31:9

   d. Jerusalem made noble. .32:1 to 33:24

     (a) In the influence of king,
         princes, and even an
         ordinary man 32:1-8

     (b) Freed from ungodly
         elements by the devour-
         ing fire of judgment
         . . . . .32:9 to 33:16

     (c) Blessed forever by reign
         of JHWH 33:17-24

III

The Nations Will Be Utterly Destroyed. Chap. 34

Conclusion

Return of the Redeemed to Zion. Chap. 35

.   .   .   .

Historical Notes

.   .   .   .

Book of Comfort

Introduction: Certainty of Restoration. Chap. 40

3. JHWH's promise is a source of strength
   for all times 40:27-31

A. Israel Returned. Chaps. 41-48

I

Returned in order to Demonstrate the Righteousness of JHWH 41:1-29
(Key verses: 41:1-2, 10, 20, 26)

1. Punishing the nations through "one
   from the east" 41:1-7
2. Restoring Israel through miraculous
   providences 41:8-20
3. Defying idols to likewise predict and
   perform 41:21-29

II

Returned in order to Bring Forth Justice to
All Nations. 42:1-17
(Key verses: 42:1, 4, 6,)

1. Through his servant 42:1-9
2. Through his own zeal 42:10-17

III

Returned in order to Provide Witnesses to His
Salvation. 42:18 to 43:21
(Key verses: 42:18, 23; 43:10, 12, 21)

1. To open the blind eyes of Israel. .42:18 to 43:7
2. To create witnesses before the nations...43:8-21

IV

Returned in order to Prove that JHWH Alone Can Save. 43:22 to 45:7
(Key verses: 43:22, 25; 44:1, 3, 6)

1. As yet, Israel does not love JHWH.....43:22-28
2. Nevertheless, he will pour his Spirit upon Israel's seed 44:1-5
3. His power contrasted with vanity of idols ....44:6 to 45:7

V

Returned in order to Work out an Eternal and Universal Salvation. 45:8-25
(Key verses: 45:8, 17, 22-23)

1. Fulfilling His purpose in Israel eternally. 45:8-17
2. Fulfilling His purpose for the world universally 45:18-25

VI

Returned in order to Take Vengeance Upon Babylon. 46:1 to 47:15
(Key verses: 46:1; 47:1,6,15)

1. Convicting transgressors in Israel......46:1-13
2. Punishing oppression and pride in Babylon 47:1-15

VII

Returned in order to Destroy Confidence In Idols. 48:1-22
(Key verses: 48:1, 4, 5, 11, 17, 20, 22)

1. Preventing false Israelites saying, "Mine idol hath done them" 48:1-11

2. Inspiring true Israelites to sing, "JHWH
   hath redeemed his servant Jacob" 48:12-22

B. Israel Saved. Chaps. 49-59

I

Saved by a Suffering Servant. 49:1-13
(Key verses: 49:4-5, 7)

1. Israel's problem: "I have spent my
   strength for naught" 49:1-4
2. JHWH's answer: a Suffering Servant....49:5-13
   (1) Who will restore the preserved of
       Israel and also be a light to the
       Gentiles 49:5-7
   (2) Who will be given "in an acceptable
       time" (a time acceptable to the will
       of God), a time of salvation....49:8-13

II

Saved by an Ensign to the Peoples. 49:14-26
(Key verses: 49:15, 19, 23, 25)

1. Zion's complaint: "Jehovah hath forsaken me" 49:14
2. JHWH's solution: an ensign to the
   peoples 49:15-26
   (1) Who will restore Zion.......49:15-21
   (2) Who will make kings her nursing
       fathers and queens her nursing
       mothers 49:22-23
   (3) Who will release her captive chil-
       dren by destruction of the mighty
       oppressors 49:24-26

III

Saved by an Inspired Teacher. 50:1 to 51:8
(Key verses: 50:2, 4, 10)

1. Israel's real trouble: failure to answer
   JHWH's call 50:1-3
2. JHWH's solution: an inspired teacher
   ....50:4 to 51:8
   (1) Who will possess the tongue of them
   that are taught, that he may know
   how to sustain with words him that
   is weary 50:4-9
   (2) Who will persuade Israel to rely
   upon his God ....50:10 to 51:8

IV

Saved by the Arm of JHWH. 51:9 to 53:12
(Key verses: 51:9,17; 52:12; 52:13 to 53:12)

1. Prophetic pleas for power........51:9 to 52:12
   (1) That the arm of JHWH will work
   miraculous deliverance as in the
   days of old 51:9-16
   (2) That Zion put on strength 51:17 to 52:12
2. JHWH's answer: the servant who saves
   by becoming a substitute........52:13 to 53:12
   (1) Who is exalted by humiliation 52:13-15
   (2) Who is strong in weakness....53:1-3
   (3) Who makes peace by suffering in
   our stead 53:4-6
   (4) Who wins honor by submission to
   injustice 53:7-9
   (5) Who saves by his death 53:10-12

V

Saved by Faith. 54:1 to 56:8

(Key verses: 54:1, 4, 11, 17; 55:1, 7; 56:3-5)

1. Prophetic exhortations unto faith......54:1-17
   (1) To sing because of the promise of
       enlargement 54:1-3
   (2) To fear not, seeing that everlasting
       lovingkindness is promised 54:4-10
   (3) To be comforted by the promise of
       protection against all enemies..54:11-17
2. JHWH's examples of faith ....55:1 to 56:8
   (1) Every one that thirsteth by coming
       to the waters without money and
       without price 55:1-5
   (2) The wicked by returning to JHWH
       ....55:6-13
   (3) Foreigners and eunuchs by choosing
       the things that please JHWH....56:1-8

VI

Saved by Judgment. 56:9 to 57:21

(Key verses: 56:11; 57:1, 3, 5, 9, 13, 15)

1. Troublesome facts concerning JHWH's
   use of heathen conquerors to execute his
   wrath upon his people ....56:9 to 57:10
   (1) Such beasts use their power greed-
       ily, ignorantly, and for their own
       gain 56:9-12
   (2) "The righteous perisheth and no
       man layeth it to heart" 57:1-2

VII

Saved by Intercession of JHWH. 58:1 to 59:21

(Key verses: 58:1, 4, 10, 13; 59:12, 16, 18, 20)

C.   Israel Glorified. Chaps. 60-66

I

Glorified by the Glory of JHWH. 60:1-22
(Key verses: 60:1-2, 7, 9, 13-15, 19-21)

Int. Israel to shine with the glory of JHWH 60:1-3

1. Because JHWH will glorify the house of
   his glory 60:4-9
2. Because the nations will serve Israel for
   the sake of Zion's glory 60:10-14
3. Because JHWH will impart the glory of
   his character to all in Zion 60:15-22

II

Glorified by the Praise of the Nations. 61:1-11
(Key verses: 61:3, 6, 11)

1. Prepared by One with the Spirit of
   JHWH upon him to be called "trees of
   righteousness" 61:1-3
2. Called by the nations "the ministers of
   our God" 61:4-9
3. Righteousness and praise caused to
   spring forth before all the nations..... 61:10-11

III

Glorified by a New Character. 62: 1-12
(Key verses: 62:1-2, 6-7, 12)

1. Called of JHWH by a new name........ 62:1-5
2. Established by JHWH as a praise in the
   earth 62:6-9
3. Made by JHWH to be "the holy people" 62:10-12

IV

Glorified by One Mighty to Save. 63:1 to 64:12
(Key verses: 63:1, 4)

1. Who works vengeance upon ungodly
   enemies like Edom 63:1-6
2. Who, as the Angel of JHWH's presence,
   carried them all the days of old and led
   them into rest despite their sin........63:7-14
3. Who will yet exercise the Father's zeal
   for redemption of his people despite
   their sin ....63:15 to 64:12

V

Glorified by a Faithful Remnant. 65:1-16
(Key verses: 65:1, 8, 13)

1. As a nation that pretends to see JHWH
   but does not really desire him, it is to receive the recompense of sin 65:1-7
2. As a nation out of which JHWH will
   bring a faithful seed, it will be preserved
   ....65:8-12
3. Only servants of JHWH to enjoy the
   glory 65:13-16

VI

Glorified by New Heavens and a New Earth.
65:17 to 66:6
(Key verse: 65:17)

1. A new Jerusalem 65:17-19
2. A new physical life: health, prosperity,
   peace 65:20-25
3. A new worship 66:1-6

VII

Glorified by a Miraculous Rebirth. 66:7-24

(Key verses: 66:7-8)

1. Delivered suddenly by JHWH 66:7-14
2. Amid judgments on all flesh 66:15-17
3. With helpers from the nations 66:18-21
4. Unto life eternal 66:22-24

TEXTUAL NOTES

1:2-9. This is not a picture of human depravity but an interpretation of Judah's invasion and desolation. The reason why JHWH should allow such judgment to come upon Judah is pointed out in 1:2. It is rebellion. JHWH has forgiven his people many, many sins and would continue to do so if they would accept his help. They, however, have refused to yield to his help or rule. Therefore, an inevitable doom is coming. Except for the "very small remnant," mentioned in 1:9, this doom would be as that of Sodom and Gomorrah.

1:10-17. This is not a condemnation of the sacrificial system but of Judah's use of it. JHWH's reference to "iniquity and the solemn meeting" at the end of 1:13 indicates that Judah had mixed iniquity with religious ritual, using ceremonies that should symbolize faith as means of doing evil. That is hypocrisy of the deepest dye.

1:18-20. The meaning of this passage is not made clear in our translations as it should be. For that reason the following one is offered:

Come ye, I pray, and let us prove each other, saith JHWH: though your sins become as scarlet, *as white as snow* they may be made: though they become red as crimson, *as wool* they may become. If ye become willing and so shall obey, *the good of the land* ye will eat. But, if ye continually refuse and so rebel, *by the sword* ye will be eaten; for *the mouth of JHWH* hath spoken.

The nature of the consequences of judgment are most beautifully stated. First, we see that these consequences depend upon the choices of those who are judged; then, that they bring purification and blessing to the obedient; finally, that they bring destruction to the rebellious. Dependence upon the choices of men calls for the translation "may be made" in 1:18. In the other two verses consequences are positively stated because the conditions are not tentative.

The purification and blessing of the obedient is enlarged in 1:21-27. Also the whole Book of Comfort is devoted to this theme.

The destruction of sinners is enlarged in 1:28-31. Also the whole Book of Judgment is devoted to this theme. At the same time the Book of Judgment constantly reveals that judgment is likewise intended to prepare remnants for salvation and glorification through the work of Messiah. This explanation shows the fitness of chapter 1 to introduce the Book of Judgment. It furnishes the motif that runs through chapters 2-35.

2:2-4. This picture of peace and glory for Jerusalem precedes long and stinging ridicule of her pride. Why? Those of Jerusalem who heard the prophet's predictions of exile for all Judah were prone to say, This cannot happen to us, for JHWH has promised to bless Jerusalem forever. This message indicates that the prophet believed in fulfilment of the promises as surely as any one, but not till after the purging of the pride of Jerusalem.

5:1-2. "My beloved" is JHWH, and "his vineyard" is Judah, as shown by 5:7. These facts are withheld temporarily to allow the song to excite interest before its crushing conclusion is revealed. Accordingly, every word down to the statement, "and it brought forth wild grapes," is calculated to create expectation of fruitfulness. The verb looked, in the clause "and he looked that it should bring forth fruit," indicates reasonable expectations. Not a simple wish, but a well-grounded hope! Then the final statement comes like a blow when a handshake is expected. This final statement should be translated "and it brought forth stinking grapes." It is a realistic picture of grapes that rotted when prepared to ripen. Could there be more effective teaching of the failure of favors alone to produce fruit and the absolute necessity for judgment to be added in order to assure future fruitfulness?

6:1-13. All the experiences in 6:1-8 lead to the instructions in 6:9-13. Thus the call is not the chief point of this message. The story of the call is an introduction that leads to the command to prophesy complete removal of the nation from the land. This fact doubtless explains why the story of the call is not at the beginning of the book. The book is not a biography. Its theme is judgment, and this message takes its place where it fits best in the line of prophecies concerning Judah's judgment.

6:9-10. This is hyperbole. It is easier to understand it intuitively than it is to explain it logically. The chief point is that the prophet is commanded to deliver a message that will harden sinners' hearts rather than save them. That is why he cries out in 6:11, "Lord, how long?" Evidently the command, "Hear ye indeed, but understand not," was not an expression of what JHWH wanted to happen, but what he knew would happen. The overstatement is purposely intended to steel the heart of the prophet for a hard task. In view of rebellious and hypocritical stubbornness, JHWH and his prophet must will to preach for the purpose of perfecting JHWH's condemnation of the reprobate as well as the forgiveness of the faithful.

6:13. Any remnant left in the land, springing up like sprouts from roots after the stock is cut down, is also to be cut down. In other words, this judgment will continue till the land be utterly desolate.

7:1-17. Again an historical experience introduces a revelation concerning judgment. The situation described in 7:1-3 leads first to an appeal to King Ahaz to have faith in God. When he hesitates, as shown by the warning at the end of 7:9, the prophet is led to offer a sign as an encouragement. In view of final refusal and hypocritical faithlessness, this offer is turned so as to condemn him. Thus the sign of Immanuel becomes the turning point in this judgment, the test upon which judgment turns toward salvation or condemnation according to the faith of the one tested. Immanuel is to be an incarnate illustration of the choice offered in 1:18-20.

To understand the faithlessness of Ahaz, we need to note a word in 2 Kings 16:5-9 concerning his dealing at this time. He was seeking aid from the king of Assyria. Evidently he thought Isaiah did not know this. Doubtless he did not want it to appear that he trusted in treaties and foreign powers rather than in JHWH; so he resorted to a hypocritical dodge, professing unwillingness to tempt JHWH when he was really trying to cover up his own perfidious acts.

"Virgin," in 7:14, though severely challenged by doubters, appears to be confirmed as a correct translation. Both usage and context support it strongly.

Nowhere else in the Old Testament is the Hebrew word for "virgin" used to describe a married woman.

The context seems to demand "virgin" in three ways: (1) as an encouragement to a faithful remnant of Israel; (2) as a wonder of wonders such as had just been offered; (3) as a condemnation of the faithless elements in the line of David.

The faithful remnant in Israel was taught to expect fulfilment of its hopes through the leadership of the Davidic line. Psalmists and prophets, both before and after this time, find the supreme inspiration of their faith in promises concerning this hope. Proof that this was uppermost in Isaiah's thinking on this particular occasion appears in 7:2, where he referred to Ahaz as "the house of David," and in 7:13, where he addressed him as "house of David." Evidently he appealed to him as one who should rely upon the promises to David. When Ahaz paraded his perfidy, another solution had to be found. Moreover, both Isaiah and Micah were giving occasion at this time for deep concern about the Davidic succession by their prophecies concerning the exile of Judah. Accordingly, both proceed to find the solution in a divine representative of the Davidic line. This is seen in Micah 5:2, Isaiah 11:1-10. Thus the virgin mother becomes the fitting link in Isaiah's thought about these matters.

The sign first offered to Ahaz was permitted to be a wonder of wonders. When JHWH said, "Ask it either in the depth, or in the height above," he removed all limitations. We naturally expect the sign that was given to be likewise a wonder of wonders. This expectation is confirmed by the description of Immanuel in 9:6 as a wonder with the attributes of deity. How could any sort of mother other than the virgin mother fulfil these expectations?

Condemnation of the faithless elements in the line of David is the requisite which seems to close the argument concerning the virgin mother. If the mother of the future representative of the Davidic line is to be a virgin, the succession will not depend upon faithless elements like Ahaz. Thus the virgin mother signifies that both the promises of God and the requisite of human faith will be sustained. Nothing less will satisfy all the teachings of this passage.

This message implies the teaching so greatly stressed later in the Book of Comfort and in all the New Testament that the judgment of every man turns upon his attitude toward Immanuel. He is the sign by which faith is tested in all times, Old Testament and New Testament times. Always those who realize their need of divine aid and trust JHWH to provide it are saved by Immanuel. Those who refuse to do so are lost.

8:1-4. This is the last introduction in the messages concerning Judah and Jerusalem. This fact seems to lump chapters 8-12 together as a prolonged final word. The significance of it appears to be largely disregarded in commentaries.

The expression, "For Maher-shalal-hash-baz," is the key to this introduction. Maher-shalal-hash-baz, meaning spoil speedeth-prey hasteth, describes the destruction of the approaching judgment as executed by an invading army. The connection in this is obvious. The meaning of "for," however, is not so obvious in this case. This may account for the neglect of our commentaries. The Hebrew word "for" may indicate relation, possession, dedication, or ascription. It may ascribe a composition to its author or a result to its cause. Ascription of a result to its cause is that which fits here. Thus the whole phrase ascribes to the judgment God has ordained a chain of results. These results are given in a remarkable series, running through chapters 8-12.

These results include great spiritual blessings, and they appear as the objective of JHWH's dealing through all his painful punishment of his people. Point two shows a believing remnant finding in JHWH a sanctuary from the storm of trouble. Point four shows JHWH's way of redeeming and restoring the believing remnant as a great messianic shoot out of the stock of Jesse which becomes a savior to all peoples. The conclusion shows redeemed Israel, restored to its own land, singing the praise of JHWH to all peoples.

Marvelous fulfilment of many of these predicted results makes a secure basis for confidence in the fulfilment of those that remain. One by one through the ages the following have been fulfilled: (1) spoiling of Damascus and Samaria by the Assyrians; (2) invasion of Judah by Assyrians; (3) overthrow of the Assyrian in the land of Judah; (4) ministry of Messiah in Galilee; (5) age-long desolation of Samaria; (6) seeking of the nations unto the Jewish Messiah. There remains restoration of a Jewish remnant through the influence of Messiah, both unto the Promised Land and unto the service of JHWH. Establishment of a worldwide, everlasting reign of peace also remains. These remain as the revealed goals toward which history marches under the providential judgment of JHWH.

14:12-20. This passage is part of a song, begun
in 14:4, which Israelites are told to sing in the day
of their restoration as a taunt to the king of Babylon
because of the breaking of his oppressive power.
Interpretation of "day-star, son of the morning," in
14:12, as referring to Satan has no basis in the text.
In 14:16 he is described as a man. In 14:20 this
satire is brought to a trenchant conclusion by refusal
of the honor of burial. Who ever heard of Satan
being buried, honorably or dishonorably?

Chapters 13-23. These messages deal with the
destiny of individual nations. They are prevail-
ingly words of doom and national destruction. Yet,
they manifest an evangelical interest in remnants.
16:1-5 is a leading example of this interest. By no
means is every foreigner condemned. Survivors are
seen.   Fugitives are objects of heart-rending concern, as in 16:11. Remnants that seek JHWH are
given assurance, as in 16:5, that the throne of Messiah will extend its benevolence unto them. In 19:
19-25 remnants of Judah, Egypt, and Assyria are
seen linked together in the future service of JHWH.

Prophecies concerning remnants indicate the
destiny of the nations mentioned. Consideration of
the ethical reasons for these prophecies is a very
profitable study. They may be found in these messages, in histories both sacred and secular, and on
the monuments unearthed by archeology.

Chapters 24-35. It is readily observed that
chapters 24-27 and chapters 34-35 deal with times
of world judgment. The destiny of individual na-

tions is no longer treated except in the cases of
Israel and Edom. There is a brief word about Moab
in 25:9-12 to illustrate the preceding word about a
feast prepared in Jerusalem for those out of all nations who fear JHWH, but this word about Moab
is not a treatment of national destiny. The cases of
Israel and Edom may be explained as typical of
godly and ungodly nations. Israel is of course the
chosen nation through which the blessings of JHWH
worship are to be extended to all who will receive
them. Edom, whose progenitor was Esau, is the
opposite in all things. These two represent those
to be saved and those to be utterly destroyed
through the judgment of the world.

The relation of chapters 28-33 is not so readily
observed. It needs to be remembered that Isaiah's
treatment of judgment always views it as a means of
purifying the elect as well as destroying the condemned. As chapter 27 pictures the glorious mission
of the purified Israel which "shall fill the face of the
world with fruit," so the chapters that follow picture
the purifying process by which Israel is fitted to
fulfil that mission.

Chapter 32 pictures the climax of JHWH's judgment of Israel. A purified remnant is ruled by a
king who reigns "in righteousness." Princes, or
secondary rulers, "rule in justice." Even "a man,"
an ordinary citizen of that realm, is a benevolent
protector of his followers. The inference is that all
who participate in the new order of that day are
led to be like their king. He is of course Messiah.

Chapters 36-39. These chapters are historical. The fact that all others in this lengthy book are prophetical sets them apart from all the rest. It makes us wonder as to the reason for their inclusion.

At least it is clear that they have the authority of accepted history and must have been included so as to bear evidence concerning other matters in the book. They are a close parallel to 2 Kings 18:13 to 20:19, so close as to indicate that they were written by the same author. Whether they were copied from Isaiah into Kings or by Isaiah from Kings, we cannot tell. In either case, they use the history of Kings to confirm certain important facts about the prophecies of Isaiah. The first section, chapters 36-37, proves the fulfilment of Isaiah's repeated prophecies that the Assyrian would be overthrown in the land of Judah. The second section, chapters 38-39, shows that this same Isaiah, the son of Amoz, predicted the Babylonian exile of Judah.

The close connection between Isaiah's prediction of Judah's exile and the prediction of restoration which follows immediately in the Book of Comfort leads to an inference of great importance concerning the authorship of the Book of Comfort. It needs to be noted that there is no indication whatever of a different time or a different author. The close connection appears to take for granted that the reader will understand that the time and the author of these two prophecies are the same. As the first section of this history looked backward and confirmed fulfilment of former prophecies, so the second section looks forward to prophecies not yet fulfilled and appears to be intended to remind readers that the prophet whose predictions have been so signally honored by fulfilment is he who delivers that which follows.

Chapter 40. The comfort called for in this verse is the comfort of JHWH's promise to restore Israel. The voice of 40:3 pictures him coming through the wilderness, as though to say all obstacles to return from exile will be overcome by him. The voice of 40:6 says his word stands forever, as though to say he will never give up till he has succeeded. These voices are probably intended to dramatize prophetic messages. The words that follow likewise portray JHWH as one whose promise cannot fail. In 40:9-11, he is a mighty One and a Shepherd, possessing the power of God to free Israel from captivity and the tender helpfulness of a shepherd to lead Israel back to his fold. In 40:12-17, he is the Creator who is able to do with his creation as he will. In 40:18-26, he is the only true God, whose word can be trusted absolutely. All these descriptions emphasize the certainty of the promise of JHWH. Accordingly, it is pictured in 40:27-31 as a source of strength to them "that wait for Jehovah," no matter how long or how terrible their exile.

This chapter serves as an introduction to all that follows in the Book of Comfort. It should, therefore, remind us that all the promises of this wonderful book are addressed to Israel. Opportunity for Gentiles to share the spiritual blessings of Israel are often pointed out. Yet, it remains true that these promises are primarily promises to Israel. Paul uses chapters 9-11 of the Book of Romans to remind Gentile Christians of this fact.

Chapters 41-48. These chapters open with descriptions of "one from the east." He is a great conqueror, raised up by JHWH. In other words, he is JHWH's means of accomplishing that part of his work described in these chapters. Afterward an altogether different means appears. Thus the use of the conqueror from the east distinguishes these chapters and marks the first major division in the Book of Comfort.

We find not merely the means of JHWH's work but also the occasion, the purpose, and the result to be sharply distinguished in each major division. Careful observation of these things is exceedingly helpful in understanding the book.

Obviously, the occasion of JHWH's work in these chapters is the Babylonian captivity and the purpose is return to the land of Israel. The result is the restoration of Israel as a nation.

It needs to be carefully observed that the result in this case involves a mixture of believers and unbelievers. The nature of the means used to accomplish this result naturally leads to the expectation of mixed spiritual consequences. Certain striking descriptions of Israel imply the same. The contrast of false Israelites and true Israelites among those returned, as seen in chapter 48, is a conclusive picture of the same. Study of this situation prepares one to appreciate the contrast in that phase of JHWH's work described in the next major division.

JHWH's means, who is named Cyrus in 44:28, is a mighty military conqueror such as was needed to break the power of Babylon. However, he is not that kind of power needed to break the power of sin. Though described with many high compliments, he is not called the servant of JHWH.

Israel is the one called the servant of JHWH in these chapters. However, the exalted service which we associate with such an one as the servant of JHWH is shown to be an ideal ministry unto which he is ordained. By no means is he said to have attained unto it, but rather to be as yet blind to it. At the same time JHWH's ordination of him is pictured as being as fixed as is the character of God, and restoration from captivity is one step in JHWH's opening of his blinded eyes.

The identity of the servant in these chapters with Israel is inescapable. It is mentioned first in 41:8 and many times thereafter. At no spot, except 42:1-9, is there the slightest occasion for questioning this identity. In studying 42:1-9, we must needs remember that the identity of the servant with Israel by the context, both before and after, requires the same identity in 42:1-9. How then can we explain the application by Matthew 12: 18-21 of parts of 42:1-9 to Jesus? The answer is that both Isaiah and the New Testament show it to be fulfilled in Messiah and in Israel, first in Messiah, then through Messiah in Israel.

The necessity for such a means of accomplishing JHWH's ordained purpose in Israel is clearly anticipated by the descriptions of the servant which immediately follow that in 42:1-9. In 42:18 he is called deaf and blind. Yet, in 42:19, he is described as "he that is at peace with me." Also, in 44:2, he is called Jeshurun, as Moses used to call Israel; and then he is told this, "I will pour my Spirit upon thy seed, and my blessing upon thine offspring" (44:3).

The most revealing of all these descriptions is that in 42:19, "he that is at peace with me." A better translation is this: he that is being made to be at peace with me, or, he that is being perfected. Four things are implied by this description: (1) the servant is now imperfect, blind, deaf, not at peace with JHWH; (2) the servant is to become perfect; (3) the change is a process in progress at the time; (4) the change is being wrought by JHWH. This description thus leaves open a place for Jesus as JHWH's future means of enlightening and perfecting his people by being what they are to be and finally making them to be as he is.

The use of the pet name Moses coined to express his hope concerning the ideal Israel is a parallel description. It means Upright One or Righteous One. Yet Israel was by no means living righteously when Moses used it. Nor when Isaiah used it! Both used it to express a hope based on the promise of God while Israel was yet largely a nation of unbelievers.

Chapter 48 describes JHWH as saying that he causes the prediction of the return to be made so that those who are "called by the name of Israel, . . . but not in truth, nor in righteousness" (48:1) will not be able to say afterward that it has been done by their idol (48:5). This also implies the presence of false Israelites after the return, and the need of a greater work of God in order to make Israel what he is ordained to be. Cyrus can send the Israelites home, but he cannot make a godly nation of them.

Chapters 49-59. The introduction of JHWH's new means comes in dramatic fashion. First, in 49:1-4, Israel speaks of his discouragement. He recounts his call only to show that it has not been fulfilled. He says JHWH has made his mouth a sharp sword, but hidden him; has made him a polished shaft or arrow, but kept him in his quiver; in other words, has made him a specially prepared instrument, yet reserved him for future use. He says, furthermore, that his own strength has been spent in vain, but concludes with this exclamation, "Yet surely the justice due to me is with Jehovah." Then, in 49:5-7, someone recounts JHWH's call to him, saying, "Jehovah . . . formed me . . . to bring Jacob again to him." It is obvious that he is to bring Jacob back to his God. The only adequate explanation, therefore, is that JHWH has appointed a new means of restoring Israel, another servant whose call is strangely identified with that of Israel, whose call is the answer to Israel's discouragement.

The dramatic fashion of this introduction is misjudged by many, seemingly because of failure to understand or accept the preceeding chapters as given. Some commentators think they see only one servant here. In translating the passage, MNT and AT arbitrarily change the text so as to make it appear that there is only one servant. MNT goes so far as to follow this up with the insertion of the word Israel in 52:13 so as to make it appear that the Suffering Servant of chapter 53 is the nation of Israel. Such pretended emendation needs to be watched very critically. It tears out the heart of Isaiah's pictures of Messiah. The failure, the absolute failure, the spiritual doom of Israel—and of all others as for that matter—apart from the help of Messiah is not seen or else is stubbornly ignored, if the teaching of this passage about Messiah's rescue of failing Israel is smothered.

As in the beginning, so all the way through this section, Isaiah makes the Suffering Servant to be the solution of Israel's spiritual problems. Each introduction presents a problem. Each message goes on to present the Suffering Servant as the solution. In other words, throughout these chapters it is he that is JHWH's means. Sin is the occasion of JHWH's work here, he the means, restoration to peace with JHWH the purpose, and redemption of a believing remnant of Israel the result. Here Messiah is made to be, more forcefully than anywhere else in the Old Testament, JHWH's guarantee of the salvation of Israel.

After Zion's complaint in 49:14, saying, "Jehovah hath forsaken me," the new servant is pictured as an ensign to the peoples. An ensign is a banner, flag, or standard. Here it is used to describe Messiah as a rallying point in the service of God for the peoples of the earth. This is a repetition of the picture given in 11:10. As chapter 11 goes on to tell how JHWH will use Gentile believers in Messiah to help restore Israel, so does chapter 49. This means that Messiah is JHWH's means of controlling all peoples so as to guide their history to a fulfilment of his promises concerning Israel and the kingdom.

In 50:1-3, the cause of Israel's trouble is diagnosed as failure to answer JHWH. Israel was prone to lay the blame on God. Therefore, he challenges them to show a bill of divorcement. Divorce means cutting off, complete and permanent separation. Thus they are challenged to produce one single word of JHWH indicating that he will at any time cut off Israel. Instead of that, the cause lies in their sinful refusal to listen to the Lord, and their exile is a sending away for a time, until they do learn to listen. But, if through ages of divine revelation and prophetic pleading they have not learned to listen, what hope can there be that they ever will? The inspired teacher, who knows "how to sustain with words him that is weary," is the answer.

Prophetic pleas for power in 51:9 to 52:12 are met by the masterpiece of all messianic prophecy in 52:13 to 53:12. It pictures the Suffering Servant as a substitute for the sinner and makes his substitutionary atonement for sin the source of all spiritual strength for sinners. It is what many love to call "the John 3:16 of the Old Testament." It is the peak toward which all previous pictures of Israel's spiritual weakness and JHWH's unbroken promises have led.

The arm of JHWH is the idea that ties together the problem and the answer in this case. As prayer is made in 51:9 for its manifestation, so the marvelous answer of 52:13 to 53:12 is expressly called in 53:1 the arm of JHWH. As the arm generally symbolizes strength, so the arm of JHWH symbolizes spiritual strength. Not force, the arbitrary and selfish use of power that characterizes the kingdoms of this world; but spiritual influence, power exercised according to the love, truth, and righteousness of JHWH! It is the saving, sacrificial, successful love of JHWH. It is the wisdom that is able to impart the truth of JHWH to his disciples. It is the righteousness that makes the children of JHWH to be like him.

Prophetic exhortations to believe in 54:1-17 are met by examples of faith in 55:1 to 56:8. Since the power of the Suffering Servant is entirely persuasive, his work depends entirely upon faith. In perfect accord with this, the examples of faith that are given dismiss every other condition of discipleship and stress faith alone. "Every one that thirsteth" may come "without money and without price." "The wicked . . . and the unrighteous" may come by simply forsaking their ways and thoughts, which implies faith in the Servant as he who alone can save. The foreigner may come. The eunuch, who represented in ancient Israel a class shut out from the full privileges of citizenship because of physical impairment, may come if only he believe.

JHWH's use of heathen conquerors to punish his people brought to mind many facts which trouble even the faithful. Some are described in 56:9 to 57:10. As shown previously in 10:5-34, 29:5-8, and 49:24-26, JHWH will finally destroy these ungodly conquerors through Messiah. Likewise, as shown in chapters 11 and 12, also in 49:22-23, he will use Gentiles converted by the manifestation of Messiah among the nations to restore redeemed Israel. These results of his dealings with the nations are emphasized again in 57:13 and 57:15. Both this destruction of some and this salvation of others furnish reasons for bringing Gentiles into the land of Israel and scattering Israel among the nations.

Finally, in 58:1 to 59:15a, the age-long spread of sin into every phase of Israel's life is painted in the blackest possible colors. If anything could prevent the salvation of Israel, this is it. After showing that every power of man has failed, the intercession of the arm of JHWH is again pointed out as conclusive assurance of his determination to save "them that turn from transgression in Jacob" (59:20).

Chapters 60-66. Everything appears under a new light in these chapters, and this new light is the glory of JHWH. 60:1 reveals this. The occasion for the Lord's work here is the shame and disgrace of Israel. His purpose is to restore Israel as a shining light in the world. His means is still Messiah, but the Glorious One rather than the Suffering Servant. The result is the glorification of Zion.

In chapters 41-48 the purposes of JHWH are emphasized above all else, in chapters 49-59 the means, and here the results. The glory of the results is described in the following glowing terms: (1) a Zion whose light is God; (2) a brotherhood including remnants out of Israel and the nations; (3) a new world order, wherein all members are righteous, which is a new creation, and whose life is eternal.

Zion is the one addressed throughout chapter 60 and frequently thereafter in this section. The Hebrew text makes this much clearer than does the English, for the personal pronouns referring to Zion are obviously feminine in the Hebrew. As shown previously by 40:9 and many other references, this Zion is the new and blessed Jerusalem that inherits the fruit of the promises of comfort. It symbolizes the ideal Israel. It stands for the believing, purified, and glorified Israel.

A spiritual brotherhood exists in this Zion which includes remnants out of Israel and the nations. 61:4-9 shows foreigners asking Israelites to be their ministers so that they may participate in the blessings of JHWH worship. 66:21 shows converted Gentiles being accepted as spiritual leaders equally with Israelites. "The middle wall of partition," referred to by Paul in Ephesians 2:14, is broken down.

A new world order appears in this Zion. All members are righteous. Service, benefit, and glory are mutual. It is a new creation.

The righteousness of all members is declared in 60:21. The setting of this verse, including verses 15-22, is a beautiful and significant passage. It is built upon ideas which first appear in 2:2-4; 4:2-6; 12:1-6; 26:1-7; and 33:17-24. It rises to a new height in picturing the perfection of the people of God in their future state. It is the forerunner of Ezekiel's picture of healing waters from the temple in Ezekiel 47:1-12, and John's picture of "the Holy city, new Jerusalem" in Revelation 21:1 to 22:5. Thus it is a foundation of our ideas about heavenly things. Yet, it is seen as existing on this earth. So is John's "city foursquare." It is a new world order but still a part of life in this world.

The mutual nature of all service, benefit, and glory in this new order is of tremendous importance. It sets up an ideal for all social relationships. All racial, national, and economic relations must be submitted to it before this new order is established. These things are illustrated in chapter 61 and in 66:18-21.

In 61:5 we see that men of other nations serve Israel with material benefits while Israelites serve them with spiritual benefits. This does not say that all Gentiles shall so serve Israelites but that

some shall. They do so by supplying the physical
need of those who serve them in spiritual matters,
even as congregations today provide for their pas-
tors. Moreover, this cannot indicate slave service
to ungodly Israelites because all those in this order
are godly people. These are called "ministers of our
God" (61:6); so they are spiritual servants whose
leadership in worship is welcomed by those who
accept their God as their own, who desire to be
taught in his ways, and who call them "the seed
which Jehovah hath blessed" (61:9). "So the Lord
Jehovah will cause righteousness and praise to
spring forth before all nations" (61:11).

In 66:18-21, Gentile converts continue to assist
Israelites, but as deliverers and some as equals in
the spiritual leadership of the kingdom of God. The
Gentile converts in this passage can be distinguished
from the Israelites by repeated references to them
in the third person. They are the ones who see
JHWH's glory (v. 18), recognize the sign set among
them, which is Messiah (v. 19), and who bring
Israelitish exiles back to Jerusalem (v. 20). Israelites are addressed in this passage in the second person, as they are throughout the book, and their seed
who are to be thus brought back to Jerusalem are
called "your brethren." This return of them by
the Gentile converts is described as "an oblation
unto Jehovah"; i.e., an offering indicating fellowship
and acceptable service. Accordingly, JHWH says,
"And of them also will I take for priests and for
Levites" (v. 21). Priests and Levites were the lead-

ers of worship in ancient Israel. When Gentiles are accepted as such, a new order has indeed come, for not all Israelites could attain to such leadership under the old order. The glory of the new is truly universal.

Not only is this glory mutually shared by all peoples, but also by men and God. When JHWH says of this Zion, "Thy God thy glory" (60:19), and, "thy people also shall all be righteous" (60:21), he adds, "that I may be glorified."

The point of supreme interest about this new order is that it is a new creation. This is described in 65:17 to 66:24 under the figure of new heavens and a new earth. 2 Peter 3:13 and Revelation 21:1 draw upon Isaiah for this figure. A new earth is described in 65:17-25 in terms of physical welfare. New heavens appear in chapter 66 as an entirely spiritual order of worship, conditioned upon "a contrite spirit" (66:2), featured finally by the miraculous rebirth of Israel as a nation (66:8), and producing life eternal (66:22).

This passage uses the idea of creation in as strict and clear a sense as Genesis 1: 1-2:3 and 2 Corinthians 5:17. Genesis 1:1-2:3 described the origin of matter, the soul of living creatures, and the image of God in man as things that God and God alone could bring into being. 2 Corinthians 5:17 gathers much New Testament teaching concerning regeneration of an individual life into a description indicating that regeneration is something that God and God alone can accomplish. Likewise, 66:1-6 teaches that the new spiritual life of an individual is to be strictly a creation of God, 66:7-24 that the miraculous rebirth of Israel as a nation will be creation of God, and the whole picture of new heavens and a new earth that this new order is something God and God alone can accomplish.

66:1 tactfully suggests that the Temple will no longer be necessary as a place for meeting with God. 66:2 proceeds to say that "a poor and a contrite spirit" will be the only condition of JHWH's favor. Jesus' word to the woman of Samaria in John 4: 21-24, saying, "neither in this mountain nor in Jerusalem ... God is a Spirit: and they that worship him must worship him in spirit and truth," is an application of this teaching. Accordingly, 66:3 goes on to picture the old order of sacrifices as an order that will have been utterly rejected. The book of Hebrews enlarges upon the reasons for this. 66:4-6 shows that the passing of the old order, so sorely feared by blind Israel, is the very thing JHWH will choose.

66:7-9 makes the rebirth of Israel as a nation a miraculous work of God like the new life of the individual with a contrite spirit. 66:10-17 shows that this will be accomplished in a time of world struggle and terrific judgments upon the nations. This builds upon the great picture of world judgment in chapters 24-35, which in turn builds upon the pictures of Obadiah and Joel. It is followed by many great pictures in Scripture, prominent among which are Jeremiah, chapter 51, Ezekiel, chapters 38-39, Daniel, chapters 11-12, Zechariah, chapters 12-14, Matthew, chapter 24, Luke, chapter 21, and the Revelation. 66:18-21 shows that the co-operation of men, the aid of Gentile converts to Israelitish exiles for instance, will have a large place in building this new world order. However, any human aid not developing out of the spiritual creations of JHWH will not belong to it. The birth in a day indicates that it will come as a surprise even to those who have greatly desired it and be the result of a miraculous intervention of God.

Life produced by these creative acts of God is described finally, in 66:22-24, as eternal. 66:22 shows it to be as enduring as is the new order itself. The worship described in 66:23 shows its quality to be godliness. In 66:24 the life of the ungodly is also shown to be unlimited in time but so cursedly miserable as to become abhorrent to the godly. The worm and the unquenchable fire of this verse reveal the everlasting condition of the people called in 34:5 "the people of my curse." This horrible contrast serves to magnify the eternal blessedness of the godly.

By way of summary, the following table will indicate the features of the main divisions in the Book of Comfort.

BOOK OF COMFORT

Chaps.	Occasion	Purpose	Means	Result
41-48	Babylonian Captivity	Restoration to Land of Israel	Cyrus	Continuance of Israel as a nation
49-59	Sin	Restoration to peace with JHWH	The Suffering Servant	Salvation of a believing remnant of National Israel
60-66	Shame and Disgrace	Restoration as a shining light in world	The Glorious One	Glorification of Zion where all believers share alike

CRITICAL PROBLEMS

IX

Prophetic Perfects in Isaiah 40-66

Sharp differences of opinion arise among students of the Hebrew text as to whether various perfects used in chapters 60-66 to describe the condition of Jerusalem are prophetic or historical. 64:10-11 is an outstanding example. A. F. Kirkpatrick explained this passage thus, "Jerusalem is in ruins."[1] He goes on to conclude that "the Babylonian exile is not predicted; it is described as an existing fact."[2] Yet, he interprets 40:1-2 as being

---

[1]Kirkpatrick, A. F., *Doctrine of the Prophets*, p. 354.
[2]Idem, p. 359.

prophetic, saying, "Jerusalem's servitude is accomplished, . . . the decree has gone forth for pardon, redemption, restoration."[3] He means that 40:1-2 describes the future as if already accomplished.

Let us note carefully that he makes 64:10-11 to describe the past, but 40:1-2 the future. Other similar passages are handled in the same way. This is typical of those views which doubt that Isaiah, the son of Amoz, wrote all. Yet, the verbs in 64: 10-11 are exactly the same as those in 40:1-2 so far as form is concerned. The only thing that can make a difference is the time indicated by the context. Even Kirkpatrick recognizes this. Therefore, it is merely an opinion he states, not an unquestionable fact, and students need to realize that there is no place for dogmatism here on either side. Accordingly, it remains true that it is possible to translate all of the Book of Comfort as referring to the future.

X

Naming of Cyrus

The naming of Cyrus, in 44:28, is another crucial problem in the interpretation of Isaiah. Many claim it is an interpolation. They think that the use of it by Isaiah, the son of Amoz, would have been unreasonable because there was no occasion for him to think of this Persian name a century and a half before Cyrus appeared on the horizon. In studying the problem it needs to be noted that the

---

[3]Idem, p. 355.

character of the one who is to deliver Israel from
Babylon grows little by little throughout chapters
41-48. Step by step the character is described as a
solution to the problem of Israel's release. The name
comes in the midst of this development. It means
the Shining One, and fits the illustrious conqueror
and emancipator already foreseen quite as naturally
as any name that could have been chosen. The
great wonder is not that such a name should be
chosen but that the prophecy about it should be
literally fulfilled. And that is pictured by the Bible
as being in the hands of God as was the naming
of Josiah and the prediction of a virgin mother for
Immanuel. If the biblical teachings concerning the
supernatural guidance of the prophets is accepted,
it is not unreasonable to accept this naming of Cyrus as an answer, both reasoned and inspired, to
problems concerning fulfilment of the promises to
Israel. The character of the Suffering Servant is developed and fulfilled in the same way.

XI

Authorship of Isaiah

There are three observations concerning the book
as a whole which incline strongly toward the conviction that all of it was written by Isaiah, the son
of Amoz. First, there is a close continuity in the
teaching from the beginning to the end. Second,
there is a climactic development which builds steadily upon messianic revelations unlike those of any
other book. Third, this teaching is crowned with a

name for God, the Holy One of Israel, which is characteristic of the book as a whole and almost peculiar to it. The first of these observations is illustrated in all the preceding treatment of the book. The second and the third will be enlarged in the theological studies to follow.

THEOLOGICAL STUDIES

XII

JHWH, the Holy One of Israel

From the time he received at the Burning Bush a vision of God's everlasting faithfulness to his promises concerning Israel, Moses interpreted the essential nature of God in terms of holiness and used the name JHWH to describe it. The psalmists, as in Psalm 89, touch this theme. Hosea, after being taught that the redeeming love of JHWH will succeed in saving Israel despite his sins, lifts the idea into a name for God, calling him in Hosea 11:9 the Holy One.

Isaiah, emphasizing the same ideas, magnifies the name Holy One of Israel so as to make it characterize the whole book. Thirty or more times is the name used. It appears in all parts of the book. It is vitally related logically to the development of the teaching. Before and after Isaiah it appears only a very few times. Thus it appears in Isaiah like a trade-mark.

The first part of this name, "the Holy One," as with Moses, the psalmists, and Hosea, stands for the essential and transcendant character of God. It describes his love, truth, and righteousness in an absolute sense that transcends our ability to comprehend, much less to emulate. This character appears supremely in chapter 45.

The second part, "of Israel," reminds us that JHWH is linked with Israel and his character revealed in his control of Israel's life, Israel's relations with other nations, and the history of the world. This is his relative and immanent nature. This involves his loyalty to the promises and the destiny of Judah. These things require the ministry of the Messiah. They lead to the belief that he is JHWH manifested unto men, God in a relative and limited sense, of course, yet truly God. Thus Messiah created hope of the universal, spiritual kingdom of God on earth as the goal of all history.

XIII

Destiny of Judah

To appreciate the sweep of Isaiah's teaching concerning the destiny of Judah, it is necessary that we observe the identity of the future, ideal Judah with the Davidic line, with Jerusalem, and with Zion. This may be seen in the following passages:

(1) Zion and Jerusalem; 1:8; 2:3; 4:3; 10:12; 33:20; 62:1-12.

(2) Jerusalem and Judah; 5:3; 10:12; 33:20; Cf. Psalm 78:68.

(3) Judah and the Davidic line; 5:7. Cf. Lion of the tribe of Judah in Revelation 5:5. With these identified, we find Judah's destiny pictured as:

Remnant Purified and Blessed

Int. Only a remnant. 10:20-22; 65:8-16.

1. Made faithful through the ministry of Messiah.
   1:21-31;   29:22-24;   30:8-9,15,18-22;   42:1-9;
   chaps. 49-59.
2. Glorified by the presence of JHWH. 4:5-6; chaps.
   60-66.
3. Being the glory of JHWH. 26:11-15; 49:3;
   60:21.

Means for the Destruction of JHWH's Enemies

Int. A threshing instrument for the judgment of
all powers, both great and small 41:15.

1. In Judah. 1:25; 28:14-22; 57:20-21; 65:11-12.
2. In Samaria. 9:8-10; 28:16.
3. In Assyria. 10:5-34; 14:24-27; 31:8-9.
4. In Babylon. 14:1; 21:10; 48:12-22.
5. In Philistia. 14:32.
6. In Damascus. 17:14.
7. In Egypt. 19:17.
8. In Edom (Dumah or Seir) 21:11-12.
9. In Tyre. 23:18.
10. In all nations. 26:11; 27:1,7; 29:5; chaps. 34
    and 35; 65:15-17.

Means of Blessing to JHWH's Lovers

Int. As promised to Abraham. 45:14-17, 22-25;
51:1-3.

1. A central influence in messianic dealings.
   (1) With men of Judah. 7:1-17; chaps. 32-33.
   (2) With Galilee. 9:1-8.

   (3) With Ephraim. 11:1-9, 16.
   (4) With the nations. 11:10-12.
2. A central place in the messianic kingdom. 2:2-4;
   4:3; 12:6; 14:1; 24:21-23; 30:19; 35:10; 59:
   20; 62:1-12; 66:20.
3. A permanently established center. 9:7; 32:18;
   33:20; 45:17; 60:20; 62:4, 65:8-10; 66:22.

XIV

Ministry of Messiah

The destiny of Judah is made to depend upon
the ministry of Messiah. He is JHWH's guarantee
that his promises will be fulfilled. As Micah fore-
saw in Micah 5:2, so Isaiah over and over foresees
him as the only character capable of bringing God
and man together, because he himself is to be a
God-man. Thus he is pictured as:

Divine-Davidic King

In chapters 1-35, many names and descriptions
are given. We find in 4:2 the Branch; in 7:14 and
8:8, Immanuel; in 9:6, a son who is to be called
Wonderful Counsellor, Mighty God, Everlasting
Father, and Prince of Peace; in 10:34, a mighty
one; in 11:1-9a, a shoot out of the stock of Jesse
upon whom the Spirit of JHWH rests; in 11:10,12,
an ensign of the peoples; in 16:5, one sitting on the
throne of David in lovingkindness, justice, and
righteousness; in 28:16, a precious cornerstone; and
in 32:1-7, a king who rules so that princes and even
ordinary citizens of his realm exercise their influence
as he does his.

The functions of Messiah in these chapters may be summarized as those of a sign, a son, a Saviour, and a sovereign. In each case, however, he is a king who is both divine and Davidic.

As a sign, he tests the faith of all, sealing the destruction of the faithless, and assuring the salvation of the faithful. He is Immanuel, with a mother from the line of David, but begotten of God.

As a son, he establishes the throne of David. When in 9:6 there comes the cry, "Unto us a son is given," it is Israel rejoicing, as families in Israel are accustomed to do, over an heir to carry on the name and to claim the inheritance. Then the verse goes on to apply names which ascribe to him the attributes of God.

As a Saviour, he creates for all peoples the peace that comes of knowing JHWH. To Judah he is a shoot out of the stock of Jesse, in other words, a new growth springing from the roots after the tree has been cut down. To the nations he is an ensign of the people, calling them to participate in his glory and his work. In both cases Messiah manifests among men the attributes of JHWH described in 11:2-9.

As a sovereign, he imparts his character to his subjects. 16:5; 28:16, and 32:1-7 tell of this work. He works like a man, but he accomplishes what God alone is able to do.

Suffering Successful Servant

In chapters 49-59, a different type of Messiah appears. He is identified with the former in 49:22 as an ensign to the peoples, but his work in Israel is quite different. We see him in 49:5-7 as a servant appointed to bring Israel back to God, yet one whom man despiseth, whom the nation abhorreth; in 50:4-9, as an inspired teacher able to sustain the weary because he is willing to suffer for them; in 52:13 to 53:12, one who becomes the power of God in sinners' lives because he bears their sins; in 55:1 to 56:8, though not named, yet obviously the cause of the faith men are exhorted to exercise; in 56:9 to 57:21, though again not named, yet by inference from other passages, the cause of the destruction of the ungodly; and in 59:16, the intercession of JHWH whereby those in Jacob that turn from transgression are saved.

The suffering in these chapters is obvious. It arises from the human side.

The success is described as that of the arm of JHWH. It arises from the divine side.

The two threads of thought are woven together in a marvelous way in 52:13 to 53:12. The passage begins by saying, "My servant shall deal wisely." The servant is of course the suffering servant of chapters 49 and 50. The Hebrew for "deal wisely" means to succeed. Moreover, the Hebrew root in its early usage, as illustrated by Genesis 48:14, meant to cross or plait. Throughout this passage, in each of the five stanzas composing its great hymn, these

two contrary trends of thought are crossed and bent
and blended so as to form a plaited line of thought
describing the marvelous work of Messiah. It appears, therefore, that the author purposed to portray
the work of the God-man as binding together divine
and human influence in a way to make him the life-
line of salvation.

The point where the two natures of Messiah are
most wondrously united is in 53:4-7, where he bears
our sins. 59:16-21 carries out this idea. He suffers
for sin as one of us, and he succeeds in making intercession for transgressors as the arm of JHWH.

Glorious-Glorifying Redeemer

In chapters 60-66, glory characterizes both Messiah and those he has redeemed. In 61:1-11, he is
the one who makes Israel worthy to receive the
praise of the nations. In chapters 63-64, he is the
one mighty to save, mighty to save from enemies
and mighty to save from sin. In 66:19, he is the
sign leading to the conversion of Gentiles, their
service as missionaries to the nations, and their help
in returning Israelites to their own land.

In these capacities the divine is most obvious.
In 61:1, the Spirit of the Lord JHWH is upon him
in such a way as to enable him to glorify Israel. In
63:7-14, as in Micah 5:2, he is identified as the
Angel of JHWH, who is identified with God in
many ways.

The human is not prominent. Yet, he is still one
intervening in human affairs as shown by 63:1-6.

Such participation in human affairs continues to make use of his human relationships.

XV

Goal of History

In chapters 24-35 world judgment is seen as a process that brings remnants out of all nations to their destiny. In chapters 60-66 it is Messiah that does this. Thus Messiah is presented as the controlling power in all history, guiding it to its goal. In this goal the following points appear:

World Judgment

World judgment appears in 24:1 in the use of the word, "the earth." The original may be translated the land or the earth. As the land it would naturally apply to Palestine, the land of Israel. In 24:1-3, there is nothing to show which way it is used. In 24:4, however, "the world," the inhabited earth, is used as a synonym. In 24:13, the phrase, "among the peoples," likewise shows that in this section it applies to the earth. On through chapters 24-35 it is world judgment that is treated as JHWH's means of setting up his kingdom. It is this same world judgment that is briefly pictured in 66:15-21 as serving to bring about a new world order. The control of this by Messiah is seen in 66:19.

Overthrow of Evil World Power

The overthrow of evil world power appears first in 24:10, then in 25:2; 27:1, 10-11; 34-35; 62:1-6; 66:15-17.

The vagueness of this description is at first baffling. As we look around, however, we realize that it was a practical necessity. The prophet and his people were being overrun by this evil world power. In prophesying its overthrow, it was good common sense to use terms understood by the initiated but not by the enemy. Moreover, this vagueness serves another wise, farseeing purpose. While the prophet doubtless thought of Nineveh, Babylon, and Egypt as standing for such world power, his words could fit any power attaining to selfish domination of the world. In this his philosophical view of history is pronounced. For these same reasons the author of the Revelation, when prophesying the overthrow of Rome, called Rome Babylon.

The characteristics of evil world power are likewise pictured without obtrusiveness. It is easy to miss them entirely. However, their importance today should be related in reverse ratio to their prominence in the text.

In 24:10, this power is called "the waste city." The adjective is the same used of the chaotic earth in Genesis 1:2, where it was described as "waste and void." We must remember, however, that in Genesis this adjective described the physical state of the earth, but here the social, ethical, and spiritual chaos of the inhabited world.

In 25:2, this power is that of "a fortified city" and "a palace of strangers." These terms fit militarism, by which utterly unsympathetic strangers rule others with an iron heel while they live in luxury.

In 27:1, this power is called "leviathan the swift serpent," which was probably intended to describe Nineveh as situated by the swiftly flowing Tigris. In the same verse it is called "leviathan the crooked serpent," which was probably intended to describe Babylon as situated beside the winding Euphrates. In 30:7, it is called Rahab, which signifies a mythical sea monster (Cf. 51:9) and was most familiar as an emblem of Egypt. In all cases, this power is pictured as a devouring beast.

In 27:10-11, there is this additional comment, "for it is a people of no understanding." This lack of understanding appears to be ignorance of JHWH and his control of all things.

In 34:6 and 63:1, this power is symbolized by Edom and the profaneness of Esau.

In 66:17, it is identified with idolatry.

Destruction of this evil world power is accomplished by Messiah. In 63:1-6, he is described as executing vengeance upon it. This appears to be the result of his providential control of history through the ages and of a crisis in a time of worldwide struggle as pictured in 34:1-5, in 66:18, and by later prophets. It is also closely related to the emergence of a new spiritual life in Israel, along with restoration to the Promised Land, as shown in 34:16 to 35:10, in 63:7 to 64:12, and in 66:7-21.

Establishment of New Heavens and a New Earth.

The new spiritual life of Israel is a part of a new world order. In 65:17 to 66:24, the terms new heavens and a new earth are used as a crowning description of this new world order. In a word they are the new Jerusalem or Zion. In detail they stand for changes of vital significance to our earthly life.

The new earth includes:

(1) A greatly lengthened span of physical existence. This is seen in 65:20.

(2) A state of security and prosperity. This is seen in 65:21-23.

(3) A reign of peace. This is seen in 65:24-25 and repeats pictures given in 2:2-4; 11:6-9; 26:1-7.

The new heavens include:

(1) A spiritual life conditioned by faith. This is seen in 66:1-4.

(2) A miraculously created state of brotherhood where service and leadership are mutually and equally shared by Jews and Gentiles. This is seen in 66:5-21.

(3) A spiritual life that is eternal. This is seen in 66:22-24 and builds upon 25:8 and 26:19.

The establishment of the new heavens and new earth also appears as a result of Messiah's providential control of history through the ages and of his intervention on behalf of Israel. It brings the life of the Holy One of Israel into the life of those who love him so that their God is their glory and they are all righteous.

This glorified and God-created Jerusalem, this faithful, brotherly, and eternal Zion corresponds to the spiritual Israel of Ephesians 2:11-21.

INTRODUCTION TO NAHUM

Parallel Reading

Eiselen, F. C., "Nahum," in *ISBE*.

Kennedy, A. R. S., "Nahum," in *HDB*.

Driver, S. R., *LOT*, chap. VI, sec. 7.

Kirkpatrick, A. F., *Doctrine of the Prophets*, chap. VIII.

Name, Authorship, and Date

The name Nahum, as shown in 1:1, is that of the author. It means Consolation and fits the message as one intended to console those oppressed by Nineveh.

The author is called in 1:1 the Elkoshite. However, his name does not appear elsewhere in the Old Testament, and the location of Elkosh is uncertain.

The destruction of Nineveh is pictured in 3:7 as future but does not seem imminent. It occurred in the period 612-607 B.C. The fall of Noamon or Thebes which occurred about 663 B.C., is referred to in 3:8 as past. It is also known that at a time about midway between these dates enemies were threatening Nineveh. For this reason 630 B.C. appears as a likely date.

Purpose and Method

Nahum undertakes to show that the vengeance of JHWH on his adversaries will bring about the destruction of Nineveh. He clothes his message with language that is poetic, powerful, and brilliant. Though brief, it attains to a high place in Hebrew literature.

OUTLINE
The Destruction of Nineveh
(Title: 1:1)

THEOLOGICAL STUDIES
XVI
Vengeance of JHWH

Nahum bases his prophecy concerning the destruction of Nineveh upon an exposition of the vengeance of JHWH in 1:2-7.

It builds upon the following background of teaching:

(1) Vengeance belongeth unto God. Cf. Gen. 4:15; Lev. 19:18; Deut. 32:35, 41, 43.

(2) It is executed upon incorrigible enemies. Cf. Num. 31:3; Psalm 7:11-16; 149:7; Isa. 34:8; 35:4; 47:3; 59:17; 61:2; 63:1, 3.

(3) It is visited upon the evil deeds of his people but not upon them. Cf. Psalm 99:8.

(4) It is executed by Messiah. Cf. Isa. 30:27-33; 63:1-6.

Nahum's exposition summarizes this teaching as follows:

(1) JHWH's vengeance is a fullness of wrath. (Cf. 1:2.) This is probably intended to teach both that the reasons for JHWH's wrath are full and certain before he executes vengeance and that the execution is complete and final.

(2) JHWH's vengeance follows mercy and is a perfection of justice upon those who despise mercy. (Cf. 1:3a.) This partial quotation of Exodus 34:6-7 shows this teaching to be an application of the ethical monotheism of Moses and an illustration of the perfect moral balance of JHWH's control of the world. This reminds us of the extension of JHWH's mercy to Nineveh as recorded in Jonah, and it emphasizes the teaching that people must bring forth the fruits of repentance to prove themselves worthy of the mercies of JHWH.

(3) JHWH's vengeance is executed through his providences. (Cf. 1:2b-6.) There is no conflict between this teaching and Messiah's control of these providences.

(4) JHWH's vengeance makes a distinction between those who take refuge in him and such as belong to Nineveh. (Cf. 1:7.)

Nahum's treatment of vengeance makes it an expression of retributive righteousness, the very opposite of the revenge which is hasty, malignant, and unjustified.

INTRODUCTION TO ZEPHANIAH

Parallel Reading

Eiselen, F. C., "Book of Zephaniah," in *ISBE*.

Selbie, J. A., "Book of Zephaniah," in *HDB*.

Driver, S. R., *LOT*, chap. VI, sec. 9.

Kirkpatrick, A. F., *Doctrine of the Prophets*, chap. IX.

Name, Authorship, and Date

The name Zephaniah, as shown in 1:1, is that of the author. It may be rendered JHWH Hides. It may reflect some experience in the author's past life. Also it may be associated with his word in 2:3, saying, "Seek ye Jehovah . . . it may be ye will be hid in the day of Jehovah's anger."

The author's lineage is traced backward to his great, great grandfather. Such emphasis on ancestry is unusual with the prophets. Also it is interesting that the name of his great, great grandfather is Hezekiah. These facts give rise to the possibility that this Hezekiah is accorded such a notice because he was King Hezekiah. The home of the author was evidently in Judah, and the reference in 1:4 to Jerusalem as "this place" seems to indicate that it was in Jerusalem.

The ministry of Zephaniah is placed by 1:1 in the reign of Josiah. The presence of such idolatry as that described in 1:3-5 and other circumstances seem to put it before the great reforms of Josiah beginning in 621 B.C. 630-625 B.C. is a suitable date.

Purpose and Method

Zephaniah devotes his book to an interpretation of the Day of JHWH. In chapter 1 he paints the

black and fearful side, then in chapters 2-3 the
bright side for those "hid in the day of Jehovah's
anger" because they seek JHWH.

OUTLINE
The Day of JHWH
(Title: 1:1)

THEOLOGICAL STUDIES
XVII

Fruits of Patience

The appeal in 2:3, "Seek ye Jehovah . . . it may be ye will be hid . . . ," is followed in 3:8 by the conclusion, "Therefore wait ye for me." When the blessings JHWH will bestow as a result of this waiting are surveyed, they make a beautiful sketch of the fruits of patience. They prepare us for the words of Jesus in Luke 21:19, "In your patience ye shall win your souls." They are:

(1) Preservation of the remnant. Cf. 2:1-3.
(2) Development of spiritual influence. Cf 3:9.
   a. Promoting universal understanding by means of a "pure language."
   b. Promoting universal worship of JHWH.
   c. Promoting universal co-operation in the service of JHWH. All will serve "with one shoulder." As we say, everyone will put his shoulder to the wheel.
(3) Purification of the remnant. Cf. 3:11-13.

INTRODUCTION TO HABAKKUK

Parallel Reading

Eiselen, F. C., "Habakkuk," in *ISBE*.
Driver, S. R., "Habakkuk," in *HDB*.
Driver, S. R., *LOT*, chap. VI, sec. 8.
Kirkpatrick, A. F., *Doctrine of the Prophets*,
chap X.

Name, Authorship, and Date

The name Habakkuk, as shown by 1:1, is that
of the prophet. It means Embrace. The reason
for its use and the whole history of the prophet are
unknown. Only one plausible suggestion arises out
of the book itself. The notes at the beginning and
end of the psalm in chapter 3, because they are
like those found in Psalms, make it appear that the
author may have belonged to the Levitical choir.
There are conflicting legends and theories, but none
of them have attained to probability.

The date should probably be judged by references in the book to the Chaldeans. Their coming,
as seen in 1:6, seems imminent yet future. A date
near the death of Josiah fits best. Thus 609 B.C. is
set.

Purpose and Method

The apparent purpose is to show how the author's trust in JHWH brought him through many
perplexities concerning JHWH's moral government
unto joy and spiritual strength as described in 3:18-
19. To do so he adopts a method that is unique
among the prophets. He portrays a dialogue be-

tween him and the Lord. He asks questions that
trouble the minds of men generally and makes
JHWH's answers to furnish solutions. This is done
with literary skill and a poetic power in chapter 3
that gives the book high literary rank.

OUTLINE

Triumph of Trust In a Time of Trouble
(Title: 1:1)

2. Further Assurances ....2:1 to 3:19
   (1) Their wickedness will like-
       wise lead to their destruc-
       tion 2:1-20
   (2) But, the righteous shall
       live by faithfulness....3:1-19
       a. Assured by the previous
          providence of JHWH 3:1-15
       b. Recognizing, trembling-
          ly, but joyfully, the ne-
          cessity for quiet waiting
          upon JHWH 3:16-19

THEOLOGICAL STUDIES
XVIII
Faith the Essential Condition of Eternal Life

Faith, as used in Habakkuk 2:4, means faithfulness to JHWH. It is the opposite of the doubt
and disloyalty toward which the questions raised
in the early part of the book might lead. It is the
fidelity and steadfastness encouraged by JHWH's
answers to those questions.

The distinction between faith as an inner principle of conduct and faith as a creed or an outward
expression of loyalty is not drawn here as Paul
draws it in Galatians and Romans. However,
Habakkuk's treatment does imply the presence of
faith as an inner principle, and Paul's quotation in
Galatians 3:11 and Romans 1:17 of his words about
faith indicates as much. Habukkuk was using his
own individual experience as an example of his

teaching. His preaching in the name of JHWH implied certain beliefs about JHWH and his plan of salvation. The sincere understanding and acceptance of these is implied by the joy and spiritual strength described in 3:18-19 as arising from them. Where such deeds of fidelity and subscription to a creed are sincere, faith as an inner principle must exist. In other words, Paul defines faith more exactly, but both emphasize it as the essential condition of eternal life.

As the outstanding Old Testament passage on faith, Habakkuk 2:4 brings to a peak the teaching of passages like Genesis 15:6; Exodus 19:5-6; 1 Samuel 15:22; Micah 7:7; Isaiah 55:1.

INTRODUCTION TO JEREMIAH

Parallel Reading

Orelli, C. von, "Jeremiah," in *ISBE*.

Davidson, A. B., "The Prophet Jeremiah," in *HDB*.

Driver, S. R., *LOT*, chap. IV.

Kirkpatrick, A. F., *Doctrine of the Prophets*, chap XI.

Name, Authorship, and Date

The name Jeremiah, as shown by 1:1, is that of the author. It may be rendered JHWH Hurls or JHWH Founds. In view of the insistence of 1:10, 12, 19 that JHWH had established him in the face of terrific opposition as a means of fulfilling his word, JHWH Founds fits best.

Notations at the beginning of chapters, scattered throughout the book, indicate the authorship of Jeremiah. One at the end of chapter 51 tells us that his words stop there. Chapter 52 is an historical appendage corresponding to 2 Kings chapters 24-25. We learn from 1:2 that the ministry of Jeremiah began in the thirteenth year of Josiah's reign, about 627 B.C. This verse also tells us that he belonged to a family of priests from Anathoth. Anathoth still exists and is on the other side of Mount Scopus from Jerusalem, about three miles distant. Evidently Jeremiah's ministry was largely in Jerusalem. 43:1-7 shows that his ministry extended till sometime after the destruction of Jerusalem, at least till 586 B.C. The last glimpse of it is among the exiles in Egypt.

Purpose and Method

The purpose of Jeremiah's prophecies was fixed by his call. We see in 1:10 that he was set "over the nations," and so to prophesy concerning other nations as well as Judah; also "to destroy and to overthrow, to build and to plant," thus to be constructive as well as destructive.

The book is a compilation of prophetic messages. These messages, as shown by chapter 36, were first delivered orally, then dictated to Baruch, a scribe, and put in their present form by him. Thus they represent the spontaneous speech of a preacher and teacher rather than the finely wrought literature of a writer.

The literary style is simple, usually obvious, sometimes labored and tedious, yet powerful as a whole and always imbued with evidences of a deeply spiritual passion. The messages usually start with some simple story or illustration and proceed with deliberate and perspicuous applications to the lives of hearers or readers. The clear-sighted and spiritual nature of the teaching is not excelled by any.

The order of the messages as they now stand is certainly not chronological. Many notes, showing times of utterance or writing, show by their mixture of dates that they are not guides to the present arrangement. The following observations are, therefore, helpful in studying the message of the book as a whole. Chapter 1, which recounts the prophet's call, serves as an introduction to all. Chapters 2-10 deal with the causes of the coming captivity of

Judah, chapters 11-23 with the certainty of the captivity, and chapters 24-29 with the completeness of it. Thus chapters 2-29 treat the coming captivity of Judah according to a clearly logical sequence. Then chapters 30-33 set forth the restoration of all Israel as assured by the unalterable promises of JHWH. Accordingly, it is as much a logical certainty as the captivity. These messages concerning restoration bring us to the heights of the book, and all remaining chapters present miscellaneous messages, some to Jews, others to the nations, all presenting deductions more or less loosely related to the main message.

OUTLINE

(Title and historical notes: 1:1-3)
Introduction: The Prophet's Call 1:4-19
Note: 1:10, 14-16. To proclaim judgment upon the nations
A.   The Coming Captivity of Judah. Chaps. 2-29

I

Causes of the Coming Captivity, Chaps. 2-10
1. Judah's own wickedness............2:1 to 3:5
   Note: 2:2-8, 13, 17, 19, 35; 3:5.
2. Refusal to repent ....3:6 to 6:30
   Note: 3:6-10 (especially v. 7); 4:1, 18; 5:1, 4-5, 19; 6:15-16, 28.
3. Trust in lies ....7:1 to 10:25
   Note: 7:4, 8-11, 14, 21-23, 28. False Worship of JHWH (*Lies to God*)
      8:5, 8; 9:3-6, 8-9, 23-26. False dealings with

men (*Lies to Men*)
10:14-16 Idolatry (Vanity and delusion, or
self deception)

II

Certainty of the Coming Captivity, Chaps. 11-23
1. The Broken Covenant ....11:1 to 12:17
     Note: 11:3, 8-11, 12:7. Because the men of
       Judah have conspired to break the cove-
       nant, JHWH "will bring evil upon them
       which they shall not be able to escape."
2. The Marred Girdle 13:1-27
     Note: 13:1-7, 9, 14, 19, 23-24, 27. As the
       girdle was marred, so will JHWH "mar
       the pride of Judah."
3. The Drought ....14:1 to 15:21
     Note: 14:1, 10-12, 15-18; 15:1-9. Prayers
       for relief forbidden
4. The Command not to Marry......16:1 to 17:27
     Note: 16:1-9, 13, 18; 17:1-4. Children "born
       in this place" and their parents "shall
       die grievous deaths."
5. The Clay in the Potter's Hand..........18:1-23
     Note: 18:1-12 (especially vv. 6, 11-12), 17.
       JHWH's plans for a nation are changed
       when the moral attitude of that nation
       changes.   JHWH is forced to "frame
       evil" against Judah because of "the stub-
       bornness of his evil heart."
6 The Breaking of the Potter's Vessel 19:1 to 20:18
     Note: 19:1-2, 10-11, 15; 20:6. "Even so will
       I break this people and this city, as one

breaketh a potter's vessel, that cannot
be made whole again."

7. Zedekiah's Inquiry Concerning the Siege 21:1-14
   Note: 21:1-7, 10, 14. Jehovah says, "I *myself*
   will fight against you . . . I will deliver
   Zedekiah, . . . his servants, and the people . . . into the hand of Nebuchadnezzar. . . ."

8. A Message to the King..........22:1 to 23:48
   Note: 22:1, 10-12, 18-19, 24-26; 23:12, 33.
   Shallum (Jehoahaz) shall die in captivity; Jehoiakim shall be buried "with the
   burial of an ass"; Coniah (Jehoiachin)
   shall die in Babylon; all false shepherds
   shall be cast off.

III

Completeness of the Coming Captivity, Chaps. 24-29

1. Two Baskets of Figs 24:1-10
   Note: 24:1-2, 4, 8. *The Residue* in Jerusalem to be given up

2. Message to All the People of Judah....25:1-38
   Note: 25:1-2, 8-11, 15, 29, 31. "This whole
   land shall be a desolation." Likewise all
   nations shall be punished.

3. Message to Worshipers in JHWH's House 26:1-24
   Note: 26:2-6. "Then will I make this house
   like Shiloh and this city a curse."

4. The Bonds and Bars ....27:1 to 28:17
   Note: 27:2-6; 28:10-14. Judah and all the

nations round about to be "given . . . into
the hands of Nebuchadnezzar."

I

JHWH's Promise, Chaps. 30 and 31

II

JHWH's Sign, Chap. 32

III
JHWH's Plans, Chap. 33

I

II

JHWH's law and their covenant to be
punished by return of the Chaldean
army and captivity

those that flee back to Judah shall be
spared.

VIII

D.   Messages Concerning the Nations, chaps. 46-51

I

II

III

IV

V

VI

VII

Kedar and Hazor. Note: 49:29. Kedar de-
spoiled 49:28-33
49:33 Hazor desolate forever

VIII

Elam. Note: 49:36, 38-39. Destruction, restoration later 49:34-39

IX

Babylon ....50:1 to 51:64
Note: 50:9, 41-42; 51:11, 27-28. To be overthrown by nations from the north.
50:23, 32, 39-40; 51:3; 9:25-26, 37, 41-44,
54-58, 64. To be utterly and everlastingly
destroyed, 50:4-5, 8, 19-20, 45; 51:5-6, 45.
Israel and Judah to seek JHWH, be freed from
captivity and saved from sin. 51:20-24.
Israel an instrument of JHWH's judgment
upon all the nations.
(Historical Notes: Chap. 52)

CRITICAL PROBLEMS

XII

Jeremiah and the Theory of Anglo-Israelism

The modern theory of Anglo-Israelism professes
to interpret many facts in the history of Israel and
in the prophecies concerning Israel's destiny. It
makes much use of Jeremiah's personal history and
the teaching of his book.

The fundamental historical part of the theory,
which claims that the Anglo-Saxon elements in

Great Britain and America are descendants of the lost ten tribes of Israel, does not touch Jeremiah. So far as Jeremiah is concerned, it may or may not be true.

Other developments of the theory do seriously affect Jeremiah. These make the present royal line of Great Britain to be lineally descended from the kings of Judah through a daughter of Zedekiah. Thus they lay a foundation for interpretation of prophecies concerning the restoration of the Davidic line as fulfilled by means of the political rule of British monarchs over the land of Israel.

This theory makes appeals for trust in a legend which says that Jeremiah left Egypt with a daughter of Zedekiah and was shipwrecked on the shores of Ireland. Later still descendants of this daughter of Zedekiah are said to have moved into Scotland and to have become members of its royal line. As history records, the royal line of Scotland has been united with that of England. So the theory links the present British line with David. At least the legend with which this chain of connections begins adds something concerning Jeremiah and Zedekiah's daughter which is not found in Kings and Jeremiah. Also it contradicts the prophecies of Jeremiah. His messages in chapter 24 and chapter 29 predicted restoration through the remnant in Babylon and destruction of the remnants left in the land. His message to the remnant in Egypt, in 44:1-14, predicted destruction of all members, "except such as shall escape," and implied that those covered by the exception would return to Judah.

Even if the legend linking the line of David with the royal line of Britain by ties of blood could be true, the use of such ties as means of fulfilling the promises to David would fly in the face of the messianic prophecies. From Isaiah and Micah on down, the prophets see the Davidic line from Solomon through Zedekiah as discredited. Because of its sin, Solomon's branch is condemned as hopeless. A God-begotten branch out of the roots of Jesse is proclaimed as the only hope. This is the meaning of the prophecies of Immanuel. In line with these are Jeremiah's predictions of a righteous Branch, whose name shall be "Jehovah our righteousness," and who will restore both Judah and Israel under the Davidic line. (Cf. Jer. 23:5-6; 30:8-9; 33:14-15.)

In this conflict with the messianic prophecies the dangerous nature of Anglo-Israelism is revealed. As it contradicts prophecies of Jeremiah which lead to man's dependence upon Messiah, so it proceeds to misinterpret prophecies of Ezekiel and others which refer directly to Messiah. Its misinterpretations tend to divert the attention of adherents toward man-centered developments and away from the only Saviour from sin.

THEOLOGICAL STUDIES
XIX
Individual Responsibility

The spiritual emphasis of Jeremiah is at its best in chapters 30-33. These chapters are the heart of his constructive work, fulfilling his call to build and to plant. It is also significant that in this work appear the chief of his brief emphases upon Messiah and one upon individual responsibility.

Individual responsibility was obscured in ancient Israel by practices which treated families as units and by teachings which dealt only with the importance of the nation. It was never contrary to the prophetical interpretations of ethical monotheism. It is implied by cries like that of Isaiah, say∙ing, "Ho, everyone that thirsteth, come ye to the waters." It is, however, given by Jeremiah an explicit interpretation and a prominence that make his word in 31:29-30 important.

This proverb in 31:29, "the fathers have eaten sour grapes, and the children's teeth are set on edge," amounted to the same as saying, The children are condemned for the sins of their fathers, or, Because of heredity, some children do not have a chance in life. Israel's use of it was intended to excuse Israel's sin.

Jeremiah's answer not merely asserts individual responsibility but predicts the acceptance of it as a doctrine in the days of the restoration.

The coming of this emphasis on individual re∙sponsibility in close connection with that on Messiah is also significant. As individual responsibility makes one's spiritual destiny to depend upon his faith, so the Messiah who saves by faith is JHWH's means of guaranteeing fulfilment of this spiritual law.

XX

The New Covenant

The finest expression of Jeremiah's spiritual teaching is found in 31:31-40. He sees a new covenant to supplant the one made at Sinai. He describes it as follows: (1) spiritual (31:31-33), (2) unanimous (31:34), (3) permanent (31:35-40).

The description of this covenant as written "in their heart" draws to a head such teachings as are found in 3:11-18; 7:1-15, and chapter 18. In its time there will be no ark, nor will the ark be remembered (Cf. 3:16). There will be no more dependence upon the ritual or outward symbolism of the Temple (Cf. 7:4). Israel will have learned the lesson of the clay in the potter's hand (Cf. chap. 18) and will know that the favor of JHWH does not abide apart from inward faith and heartfelt trust. All this is an expansion of Isaiah 66:1-4.

The description of this covenant as unanimous is likewise a restatement of teaching found in Isaiah 60:15-22.

The description of this covenant as permanent builds upon the teaching of all the prophets but receives a peculiarly clear and powerful emphasis. The conditions named in 31:36-37 are intended to show that this covenant will never be broken as was the one at Sinai. Jeremiah's greatest contribution is his use of the term, "new covenant," to describe this. He makes it express the unimpeachable sanctity of the promises of JHWH concerning the restoration of Israel as a nation.

Jeremiah's descriptions leave no room for doubt that this new covenant is made with Israel as a nation. It replaces the one made with the nation at Sinai. The cessation of Israel as "a nation" is definitely brought into question and denied in 31:36. Literal restoration to the Promised Land as a fruit of it is described in 3:18; 7:7; and 31:38-40.

When Gentiles apply this covenant only to the Spiritual Israel that is composed of Jews and Gentiles, denying any peculiar reference to the Jewish remnant, they obscure part of the facts. It is a classic illustration of the spiritual relations which eternally bind JHWH to all men who trust him, but it is primarily an assurance of Israel's restoration as a nation. The two chapters immediately following build upon this fact and should be carefully noted in this connection.

INTRODUCTION TO LAMENTATIONS

Parallel Reading

Orelli, C. von, "Book of Lamentations," in *ISBE*.
Selbie, J. A., "Book of Lamentations," in *HDB*.
Driver, S. R., *LOT*, chap. X, sec. 3.

Name, Authorship, and Date

As a name for the book of Lamentations, Jews have used the word "How," which is at its beginning, or the word "Funeral Hymn," which describes its character. From the latter word, Lamentations has come to us through the LXX.

Jewish tradition has consistently attributed the book to Jeremiah. Though some critics now question his authorship, no sufficient reason seems to have been produced. The personal experiences of chapter 3 seem to fit Jeremiah.

The time was soon after the fall of Jerusalem, so about 586 B.C.

Method and Purpose

Each of the five chapters is an elegy. The first four make an acrostic use of the alphabet. There is no such progress of thought as to indicate a clear outline. The purpose probably was to give free vent to grief over the national catastrophe of Jewry and to require only the elegance of a hymn of mourning for its expression. There are many repetitions and some expressions of seeming despair, as in 5:22, but the justice of JHWH is clearly recognized in 1:18 and 3:39, and JHWH is shown in 3:21 -39 to use suffering as a means of purification and future blessing.

INTRODUCTION TO EZEKIEL

Parallel Reading

Moller, Wilhelm, "Ezekiel," in *ISBE*.
Skinner, J., "Ezekiel," in *HDB*.
Driver, S. R., *LOT*, chap. V.
Kirkpatrick, A. F., *Doctrine of the Prophets*, chap. XII.

Name, Authorship, and Date

The name Ezekiel, as shown by 1:3, is that of the author. It means God Strengthens. There may be an intimation of this meaning in the vision of chapter 1, which serves as an introduction to the book. It is a vision of JHWH's glory reigning over this time of trouble so as to sanctify it to the spiritual strengthening of his people and to get glory to himself.

The references to the authorship of Ezekiel are so many and so clear that there has been almost no attempt to challenge the genuineness of the book. The prophet both delivered (Cf. 11:25) and wrote (Cf. 43:11) his messages. He speaks in the first person throughout the book, giving ready indications of authorship and unity.

We learn from 1:2 that Ezekiel's ministry began five years after he was carried into captivity along with Jehoiachin. That makes the beginning about 592 B.C. 29:17 shows that it extended at least till the twenty-seventh year of captivity, or about 570 B.C.

Method and Purpose

Ezekiel makes much use of illustrations and symbolic figures. The vision of chapter 1 is typical of this style. At times it is used to unveil the future, as in chapters 37-48. In this way it becomes a type of literature called apocalyptic. Touches of it are found in Joel and in Isaiah, chapters 24-27. Ezekiel brings it to a high point of development and sets an example followed by Daniel, Zechariah, and the Revelation. In all these cases it is used to predict for the initiated, in terms not understood by their conquerors, the final overthrow of evil world power and the establishment of the kingdom of God.

Some parts of the book of Ezekiel are verbose and tedious. However, the chief cause of our listlessness in reading is due to failure to grasp the purpose of its elaborate illustrations.

As a whole, the book of Ezekiel is carefully planned, closely unified, and exalted in its teaching. The most obvious turn in the teaching comes in chapter 33, after news of Jerusalem's fall reached the prophet. Before the fall he interpreted the exile of Judah and the judgment of the nations, afterward the restoration of Israel. In all parts developments are explained with reference to the glory of JHWH, making it the theme of the book. To understand matters in Ezekiel, one must understand the relation of those matters to the glory of JHWH.

In chapter 1, "the appearance of the likeness of the glory of Jehovah" is seen on a throne, reigning over all creation. This vision came by the River

Chebar, a Euphrates canal where the Hebrew captives lived. Thus the vision may be interpreted as indicating that JHWH was controlling the captivity so as to get glory out of it for himself. It introduces the message of the entire book.

In chapters 2-24, the effects of this message upon Israel are shown. First, they are bitter, then sweet, as when the prophet ate his roll according to 2:8 to 3:3. They include siege, famine, exile, and destruction. A climax is reached in the departure of the glory pictured by chapters 8-11. First, it departed from the cherub in the holy of holies, which signified the presence of JHWH (Cf. 9:3 to 10:4). Then, it departed from the threshold of the Temple (Cf. 10:18-19). Finally, it departed from the east gate to stand upon the mountain on the east side of the city, which is the Mount of Olives (Cf. 11:22-23). In the end, however, these effects are seen as accomplishing forgiveness through judgment. The fine spiritual insight revealed in this ought to relieve the boredom we sometimes feel in reading lengthy chapters and the repugnance we feel sometimes when looking at pictures of the disgraceful nakedness of sin. The prophet faces the stark realities of sin and sees that terrific measures are necessary to burn it out of Israel.

In chapters 25-32, judgment and vengeance upon the nations are likewise means whereby JHWH makes his glory to be recognized. This is shown by the conclusion, "And thou shalt know that I am Jehovah." (Cf. 25:7.) This conclusion recurs constantly in these chapters, as in all other parts of the book.

In chapters 33-48, everything builds in similar ways to a crowning point, which is the return of the glory to dwell "in the midst of them forever." All of chapters 40-48 must be interpreted in the light of this highly spiritual conception. The glory appears as Messiah himself. All effects are consonant with his universal, spiritual rule.

OUTLINE
GLORY OF JEHOVAH
Historical Note: 1:1-3

THEOLOGICAL STUDIES

XXI

Individual Responsibility

The word of Jeremiah 31:29-30 about individual responsibility is very effectively enlarged by Ezekiel in chapters 18 and 33. Both chapters expound this text, "Everyone according to his ways" (Cf. 18:30; 33:20).

Chapter 18 uses many illustrations to lead to this conclusion in 18:20, "The soul that sinneth, it shall die." Turns given to this principle in 18:21 and 18:24 show that it is the final, fixed choice of each individual that determines his destiny.

Chapter 33 shows that JHWH makes the weight of this responsibility heavier still by adding grace to justice in the appointment of watchmen to warn the wicked.

XXII

Certainty of Israel's Restoration in the Land of Israel

In chapter 36, especially verses 22-38, by interpreting the restoration of Israel as assured for JHWH's sake, Ezekiel emphasizes the certainty of a literal and permanent restoration in the land of Israel. On one hand this interpretation removes any thought that restoration to the land must wait upon the spiritual regeneration of Israel. On the other hand it leads to the conclusion that the return to the land will be used as a means of bringing about spiritual regeneration. Accordingly, we find that the giving of "a new heart" and "a new spirit," described in 36:25-31, follows the gathering "from among the nations," described in 36:24. This becomes quite important in view of the fact that Daniel and Zechariah later magnify this order of events. Thus they make way for rejection of Mes-

siah at his first coming and link his final recognition
by Israel with a time when Israel is cut to a remnant
and threatened with annihilation by the nations.

XXIII

Gathering of the Nations Against Israel

In Ezekiel, chapters 38-39, the gathering of the
nations for war against Israel is described. The
pictures of Joel, chapter 3, and Isaiah 66:18 are
enlarged, the following points being added:

(1) The leader is Gog, prince of Rosh, Meshech
and Tubal. (Cf. 38:2.)

The identification of names with people of today
is extremely difficult. Whatever probability there
may be as to identification with ancient peoples, the
tracing of connections down to modern times remains very uncertain.

(2) The source of the movement is the utter-
most part of the north. (Cf. 38:6,15; 39:2.)

(3) The time is the latter years. (Cf. 38:8.)
This expression, the latter years, seems to correspond
to the latter days of Isaiah 2:2 and Micah 4:1, all
describing events in the later parts of the messianic
age.

(4) The motive is plunder of the unprotected
wealth of JHWH's people. (Cf. 38:10-13.)

(5) The fate of the movement is destruction by
means of a world-shaking manifestation of JHWH's
presence. (Cf. 38:14 to 39:6.)

(6) The effect upon Israel will be recognition of the holy name of JHWH. (Cf. 39:7-24.)

(7) The blessing of Israel will be permanent. (Cf. 39:25-29.) In general, this picture foreshadows the final desperate struggle of heathen world powers against the worshipers of JHWH. It is seen again in Daniel, in Zechariah, and finally in Revelation 20:7-10, which puts these events at the end of the Revelation's description of the millennium.

XXIV

Earthly Reign of Messiah

Ezekiel's treatment of the glory of JHWH draws out clearly certain oft-implied distinctions which identify its earthly manifestation with Messiah. In general, this manifestation of the glory has the same essential characteristics as the God-man of Isaiah. Also its reign over the captivity and its judgment of the nations correspond to the activity of the messianic king in Isaiah. In chapters 40-48, however, we come to a picture of the messianic age which goes beyond Isaiah in clarifying the spiritual nature of Messiah's earthly reign. Three facts of transcendant importance to the kingdom of God emerge from these passages, as follows: (1) the kingdom's heavenly conditions are established on earth; (2) the supreme ruler of the kingdom is divine; (3) the throne of this supreme ruler is spiritual.

There are several strange, striking, and instructive features of chapters 40-48 which seem to have been adroitly planned to signify these lessons concerning the kingdom. They are: (1) substitution of the throne of the glory for the ark; (2) closing forever of the east gate through which the glory returns; (3) waters flowing from beneath the Temple which bring healing wherever they come; (4) division of the land in straight, narrow strips.

40:1 to 43:12 tells of the substitution of the throne of the glory for the ark. The enlarged measurements of the Temple prepare us for this by indicating that it will be a temple with a new form. The reader is further prepared to look for this new form by a remark in 41:21, which says that "the face of the sanctuary" had the appearance of the Temple; i. e., the former appearance (Cf. footnote in ASV). If the face of the sanctuary appeared as it did formerly, then what about the inner part? 43:11-12 adds a reminder that its form should be carefully observed. The omission of any mention of the ark goes a step further. The survey of the man with the measuring rod pretty thoroughly covered the Temple area and the Temple, gradually converging on the inner sanctuary, which was mentioned several times as the separate place. His survey, however, omitted from the outer sanctuary the table of shewbread (presence-bread) and the candlestick with seven lamps. Most significant of all, it omitted all the furniture of the inner sanctuary. The furniture of the inner sanctuary had formerly included the ark, the center of all the ancient Temple service, the chief symbol of the presence of God. Those symbols which the people were most prone to think of as substitutes for the presence of God were left out. It is possible that the elaborate description of other parts of the sanctuary was consciously intended to make this omission attract attention. Finally, the glory filled this inner sanctuary and set up his throne there.

This picture of the throne of the glory is in accord with Isaiah 66:1-4; Jeremiah 3:16; 7:1-7. All these words tell us simply that Israel's reliance upon the outward forms of the Temple and the ark are to cease utterly.

43:13 to 46:24 tells us of the closing of the east gate after the return of the glory and its effects upon the life of Israel. That the closing of the gate indicates the abiding of the glory seems quite obvious. To appreciate the relation of the glory to the life of the people, we need to note facts scattered through this lengthy section. There are people, priests, and princes, but all are sanctified by the presence of the glory. Thus there are religious and political leaders ruling over the people along with the glory; so the rule of the glory is a spiritual rule in and over all. Even the prince still offers sin-offerings and is to die as a mere man; so there is still a temporal and sinful order engulfing all men, and they are dependent upon the glory for victory over sin and death.

47:1-12 draws the picture of healing waters. Their connection with the Temple, which we must needs remember is the throne of the glory (Cf. 47: 1-2), their rapid increase (Cf. 47:3-5), and their healing powers (Cf. 47:6-12) should make their spiritual nature obvious to all. When it is said that these waters bring healing "whithersoever the river cometh" (47:9), the spiritual blessings are shown to be for all peoples. Accordingly, when John draws a parallel picture in Revelation 22:1-2, he says the healing is "for the nations."

47:13 to 48:35 describes the division of Israel's inheritance. An odd feature appears in 48:1-7, the portions of the tribes being long, narrow strips, running straight from one side of the land to the other. No attempt is made to follow old tribal boundary lines. No regard is paid to natural geography. The lines run "from the east side to the west side,"—no matter what the preferences of the people! no matter where the mountains, rivers, and plains! It is inconceivable that people will settle on the land like that. Thus we are led to conclude that the author never meant to describe exact geographical locations, but rather to symbolize equal sharing by the tribes in the restored life of Israel. This plan is parallel to that adopted in Revelation, chapter 7, where the 144,000 saved out of Israel are divided into 12,000 for each tribe.

This great picture of spiritual blessings, including all of chapters 40-48, is concluded by saying of Jerusalem, "The name of the city from that day shall be, Jehovah is there." This statement brings to a head the visions of the glory which run through the book from the vision of chapter 1. The key to them seems to appear in 1:28. When the power on the throne is described in 1:28 as "the appearance of the likeness of the glory of Jehovah," a distinction is drawn between the likeness and the glory, yet they are identified in their rule over creation. This distinction and this identity together furnish an explanation for the name, "Jehovah is there."

Inasmuch as the ruler on the throne is the appearance of the glory, he is distinct from the glory. He appears to men, and his appearance is that of a man according to 1:26, while all Scripture teaches that men cannot see the face of God, or comprehend the fulness of the glory.

Inasmuch as this ruler on the throne is also the likeness of the glory, he is identified with the glory. He sits on the throne of the glory, exercising the prerogatives of God in ruling over all creation. He is accompanied by the cherubim, the living creatures of chapter 1 being cherubim according to 10:20, and all Scriptures present the cherubim as accompaniments of the presence of God. In the visions of chapters 8-11 and of chapter 43, he departs from and returns to the holy of holies, which was God's place for meeting with his people. In these latter visions, care is taken to say that the glory is the same glory seen in the first vision (Cf. 8:4; 43:3), but distinctions are omitted and identity is stressed by calling the one on the throne the glory of the God of Israel (Cf. 8:4; 9:3; 10:18-19; 11:22-23; 43:2, 4-5). Finally, in 44:2, the fulness of identity within the limits of physical manifestation is affirmed by using the full name, "Jehovah, the God of Israel."

We are brought here face to face with a description which precisely parallels the following description of Jesus Christ given by Paul in Colossians 2:9, "In him dwelleth all the fullness of the Godhead bodily."

What more positive preparation could there be than the foregoing for these words of Jesus to Philip, "He that hath seen me hath seen the Father" (John 14:9)? These words are wondrously expounded in the prayer of John, chapter 17, as Jesus says:

"Father, the hour is come; glorify thy Son, that the Son may glorify thee: even as thou gavest him authority over all flesh, that to all whom thou hast given him, he should give eternal life. And this is life eternal, that they should know thee the only true God, and him whom thou didst send, even Jesus Christ. I glorified thee on the earth, having accomplished the work which thou hast given me to do. And now, Father, glorify thou me with thine own self with the glory which I had with thee before the world was. I manifested thy name unto the men whom thou gavest me out of the world: . . . Neither for these only do I pray, but for them also that believe on me through their word; . . . And the glory which thou hast given me I have given unto them; that they may be one, even as we are one."

INTRODUCTION TO DANIEL

Parallel Reading

Wilson, R. Dick, "Book of Daniel," in *ISBE*.
Curtis, E. L., "Book of Daniel," in *HDB*.
Driver, S. R., *LOT*, chap. XI.
Pusey, E. B., *Daniel the Prophet*, chap. II.

Name, Authorship, and Date

There is no title for the book of Daniel in the text. Daniel's name is very justly given to it by us, however, because he is its dominating character.

Much heated controversy arises over the authorship. The last six chapters, and particularly the last three, are the center of the storm. They profess to be predictions of future events. Also they profess to be the work of Daniel, using the first person instead of the third, which appears in the first six. Many claim that it is contrary to the nature of prophecy to give such a wealth of details concerning future events as is found here. Others say that no limits can be put upon the ability of God to reveal the future. It is true that chapters 10-12 are outstanding as to the sharp details of the future picture. However, they are not so very much more so than Ezekiel, chapters 38-39. They are an extension of those chapters and of many other preceding pictures of the future. Moreover, to say that a professed prophecy is really a description of past events is to charge that the author deliberately misrepresented the facts. Such a charge is a charge against the integrity of the Bible. Conservative students, therefore, accept Daniel as the author of the whole, or else as the source of manuscripts and information which have been put together by a young contemporary.

The date is put near the end of the sixth century B.C. by those who accept Daniel as the author. Others usually look upon chapters 10-12 as reflecting events in the reign of Antiochus Epiphanes and place the book about 165 B.C.

Method and Purpose

It is an interesting fact that 2:4 to 7:28 is written in Aramaic, while the remainder is in Hebrew. However, efforts to show any connection between this use of languages and the plan of the book do not seem to have been successful.

The book as a whole magnifies God's providential control of the world. Chapters 1-6 recount personal experiences which illustrate God's care of faithful Israelites in exile and his use of them to work out the judgment of other nations. Chapters 7-12 build upon the interpretation of Nebuchadnezzar's image-dream in 2:31-45 so as to show that God's judgment provides for the supplanting of world empires by the kingdom of God. The succession of world empires is a feature. At the heart of the matter lies the provision seen in chapter 9 for the finishing of transgression in Israel by the cutting off of Messiah, another destruction of the Temple, and the continuance of desolation unto the full end.

OUTLINE
I
Experiences of Daniel and his Companions,
Chapters 1-6

1. Purpose not to defile themselves with
king's dainties 1:1-21
   (1) Put in training for king's service 1:1-7
   (2) Permission not to defile themselves
made to depend upon effect on
physical fitness 1:8-16
   (3) They excell in physique, wisdom,
and understanding 1:17-21

2. Interpretation of Nebuchadnezzar's
image-dream 2:1-49
   (1) Chaldeans doomed for failure to reveal forgotten dream 2:1-13
   (2) Dream revealed through Daniel 2:14-45
   (3) King acknowledges greatness of
Daniel's God 2:46-49

3. Deliverance of companions from fiery
furnace 3:1-30
   (1) They refuse to worship a golden
image 3:1-12
   (2) Delivered by one "like the son of
the gods" 3:13-27
   (3) Nebuchadnezzar again acknowledges
God of Israel 3:28-30

4. Counsel to Nebuchadnezzar concerning
pride 4:1-37
   (1) Dream of a great tree cut down
troubles the king 4:1-18

II

Visions of Daniel, Chapters 7-12

THEOLOGICAL STUDIES
XXV
Succession of World Empires

Daniel's experience in interpreting the image-dream of Nebuchadnezzar laid a foundation for all his teaching about the world empires that would succeed that of Babylon. Each of the four visions in chapters 7-12 builds upon the interpretation of that dream. The first pictures four world empires before that of Messiah, and these are generally interpreted as being the same four seen in the dream. The remaining visions reveal details concerning certain ones without reviewing the whole list, but these are understood as belonging to the original four. The naming of these four becomes a matter of widespread interest. Comparison of all passages favors the following:

(1) Babylonian. This is indicated by Daniel in 2:38. 7:4 gives another description of the same. The dual nature of the lion-eagle, pictured in 7:4, was anticipated by Jeremiah. Jeremiah 4:7; 49:19; 50:17, 44 describe Nebuchadnezzar as a lion. Jeremiah 49:22 pictures him as an eagle.

(2) Medio-Persian. Some have listed the Median and Persian empires separately. Such reckoning makes the fourth to be the Greek rather than the Roman. It is usually followed by those who believe that the professed visions were not visions at all but descriptions of events already past. Those holding that opinion must find four empires before the Roman, because the time of writing which fits

their theory is the reign of Antiochus Epiphanes, when the Greek Empire had already split into four parts and the one headed by Antiochus had already manifested its hatred of the Jews.

Recent historical and archeological studies of Babylon have tended more and more to confirm the theory that Darius the Mede (Cf. 5:31) ruled over Babylon for about two years as a representative of Cyrus, but not as the supreme ruler of the realm, while Cyrus completed his conquest of outlying districts. Accordingly, Cyrus returned after those two years and assumed the rule. This makes the rule of the Medes and the Persians one from the beginning.

Daniel's description of the second beast as a bear (Cf. 7:5) fits the Persian rule as a whole very accurately. As a bear is heavy and ponderous, yet terribly destructive when it strikes, so were the Persian fighting forces to a notorious degree after Cyrus. The three ribs in its mouth correspond to the three kingdoms swallowed by the Medio-Persian, the Babylonian, the Lydian, and the Egyptian.

According to this interpretation, the bear of the first vision corresponds to the ram of the second vision. The ram is designated in 8:20 as Persia.

(3) Greek. Daniel's description of the third beast as a leopard (Cf. 7:6) likewise fits the Greek power very accurately. As the leopard is one of the swiftest and fiercest of beasts, so were the conquests of Alexander the Great. The wings doubtless symbolize the same. The fact that there were four wings and also four heads corresponds to division of

Alexander's empire into four parts and to the intelligence of the Greek Kingdom, which has always been recognized as a dominant feature of its influence.

Accordingly, the third beast corresponds to the he-goat of the second vision.

The fourth vision develops details of the struggles between divisions of the Greek Empire with special reference to efforts to destroy the Jews and the sanctuary.

(4) Roman. Daniel called this one a beast but did not name it. Biblical usage makes the word beast describe ungodly world power. To that extent the fourth kingdom is like the others. Its differences, however, could not be symbolized by those of one particular beast. Its strength is its most prominent characteristic, three forceful terms being used to describe it. Moreover, after devouring and breaking its victims, it stamps the residue, as abiding in its rule over their remnants. This corresponds to the nature of the Roman Empire, which by establishing a rule by law incorporated the remnants of nations it conquered and perpetuated its rule far beyond the measure of preceding world empires.

The ten horns of the fourth beast correspond to the ten toes of the image in chapter 2. As the words king and kingdom are used interchangeably in these visions (Cf. 7:23), so these ten horns are taken to be ten kingdoms arising out of the Roman, and the little horn of 7:8, 20-22, 24-26 to be the representative of an eleventh kingdom arising among those ten and provoking the catastrophic struggles of the end-

time by blasphemy and war against the saints. He
appears to correspond to the king described in 11:36-
45. This one is similar to the one of 8:23-26 in efforts to destroy the Chosen People and worship of
the true God but not in other particulars, especially
his contemptuous disregard of all gods and conse-
quent magnifying of himself above all gods (Cf.
11:37). The one in chapter 8 belongs to the end of
the Greek kingdom (Cf. 8:17, 23), this one belongs
to the end of the age dominated by the powers of
this world, or the Gentile age. This one corresponds
to the Anti-Christ of the New Testament.

The destruction of this last beast is shown by
11:45 to 12:3 to be in the land of Israel, suddenly
in a time of unprecedented trouble, by miraculous
intervention of a messenger from God called
Michael. The results of this event are to be deliverance of the true children of God, resurrection of
many from the dead, and the shining of those that
turn many to righteousness. This picture is a link
between Ezekiel, chapters 38-39, and Zechariah,
chapters 12-14.

XXVI
Messiah's First Coming

Daniel's vision of the seventy weeks in 9:24-27
describes a cutting off of Messiah Prince which
sharply distinguishes his first coming from the time
of his reign over Israel. This passage is the first
in the Old Testament to use the word Messiah. We
have need to watch ourselves in our use of the word.
We use it in connection with all descriptions of
Messiah, even from the beginning, and we lead our-

selves to suppose that the authors of these descriptions thought of one person in all cases. That was not so. This passage, however, by calling him Messiah Prince and also saying that Messiah ("the anointed one") will be cut off, contemplates one and the same person. Moreover, it marks clearly the purpose, time, and results of his first coming.

The purpose is seen in 9:24. Six separate descriptions are given. All describe one consuming purpose. That purpose is atonement for sin. The first three deal with the removal of sin and its consequences. The fourth turns to the positive side, the bringing in of "everlasting righteousness." The fifth, which is "to seal up vision and prophecy," does not mean to make to cease, but to put upon it the seal of approval and fulfilment. The sixth would best be translated "to anoint a most holy one." It describes the anointed one, Messiah, as that most Holy One. It points to him as the reality so long symbolized by the holy of holies, the reality that is to supplant the symbol according to Ezekiel, chapters 40-48.

The time is seen in 9:25.

The seventy weeks are literally seventy periods of seven. Evidently they are seventy weeks of years. Weeks of years are as familiar to Hebrew thinking as weeks of days. This vision came in the first year of Darius, the Mede (Cf. 9:1), immediately after the Medes and Persians had conquered Babylon, when the prospects of fulfilment of Jeremiah's prophecy concerning seventy years led to consideration of the time necessary to "finish transgressions" (Cf. 9:2). Deep consciousness of Israel's sin led to conviction that the period of time needed to "make an end of sins" must be a prolonged one (Cf. 9:3-23). Seventy weeks of years is the interpretation that fits these circumstances.

The seventy weeks are divided into groups of seven, sixty-two, and one. Reasons for this division, at least suggested ones, are necessary for an interpretation of the passage. The seven (49 yrs.) and the sixty-two (434 yrs.) are linked together as a total of the time (483 yrs.) to elapse between "the going forth of the commandment to restore and rebuild Jerusalem" and the time of "the anointed one, the prince." The reason for dividing this total seems to be indicated by the explanation following, which indicates that fulfilment of the order to restore would come "in troublous times." The seven (49 yrs.) may naturally be considered as fitting the period following the order to restore and within which the rebuilding would take place. The sixty-two (434 yrs.) then fits the period between the rebuilding and Messiah. Thus the one (7 yrs.) is related to the time of Messiah himself.

The time of the command to rebuild Jerusalem is a difficult problem. Four possibilities are usually considered: (1) first year of Cyrus, 536 B.C., when he commanded restoration of the Temple (Cf. Ezra 1:1-3); (2) third year of Darius I (Hystaspes), 518 B.C., when he continued the order of Cyrus (Cf. Ezra 6:3-8) (3) seventh year of Artaxerxes I (Longimanus), 457 B.C., when he not merely gave gifts "to beautify" the Temple (Cf. Ezra 7:8, 12-23, 27) but

also commanded Ezra to set in order the life of the
people in Jerusalem (Cf. Ezra 7:24-26); (4) twen-
tieth year of Artaxerxes I, 445 B.C., when he authorized Nehemiah to rebuild the walls of Jerusalem
(Cf. Neh. 2:1-8). The third of these seems to fit
best. On the basis of the usually accepted dates
given above, 483 years after 457 B.C. brings us to
A.D. 27. If the birth of Christ is reckoned some
three to four years before A.D. 1, he was about thirty
years old in A.D. 27 and manifested himself in bap-
tism at that time.

Caution ought to be observed as to the intention
of the prophet concerning the use of these dates.
He may never have intended that his figures be ap-
plied with mathematical exactness. Prophecy as a
rule avoids dating of the future. On the other hand,
it builds always upon developments of moral principles. These facts incline to the conclusion that
Daniel's figures should be accepted as approxima-
tions, intended to illustrate proportionate relations
between the length of the Babylonian captivity and
the time required for the manifestation of Messiah.
If the coming of the Wise Men of the East to Bethlehem at Jesus' birth was moved first of all by
Daniel's prophecy, their conduct becomes evidence
of what we are saying. Their expectation evidently
looked toward a certain period of time but not a time
calculated with mathematical certainty. They were
dependent upon another providence, the appearance
of the star, for more exact guidance as to time.

The relation of the one week (7 yrs.) to the
other is a matter that provokes wide differences of

interpretation. All see it as connected with the work of Messiah, but some make it fit the first coming, others the second coming. Those applying it to the first coming make it to follow the sixty-nine weeks immediately. Those applying it to the second coming detach it from the sixty-nine, thinking there is no indication in Daniel's words as to when it will begin. Mention at the beginning of the passage of the seventy weeks as a unit naturally leads to the conclusion that they form an unbroken stretch. Then the absence of any statement thereafter concerning separation seems to be sufficient warrant for clinging to the first of these interpretations.

The results of the first coming are seen in 9:26-27. They reach beyond the last week, even unto the "full end" and so to the second coming, but all are consequences of the first coming and its tragic end, and thus are connected with the last week. They are: (1) cutting off of Messiah; (2) destruction of "the city and the sanctuary"; (3) desolations, which will extend to the full end.

The cutting off of Messiah is followed in 9:26 by the destruction of Jerusalem and the Temple, then by desolations unto the end. This order indicates that we may have a series of consequences here, each growing out of the other. The order of events in 9:27 appears to be the same. In that case, the he of 9:27 who makes "a firm covenant with many for one week" is "the anointed one" of 9:26 in his work with his disciples before being cut off; the cessation of "the sacrifice and oblation," which is

the main point of concern in the destruction of
Jerusalem and the Temple, corresponds to the cutting off of Messiah in the midst of the week; also
"the one that maketh desolate" is "the prince of the
people that shall come," whose work follows "upon
the wing (or pinnacle) of abominations." Accordingly, the destruction of the city and sanctuary was
accomplished by Titus in A.D. 70, and the pinnacle
of abominations is to be reached in the work of
Anti-Christ, but both are simply items in the desolations that continue till the full end.

This interpretation makes the whole prophecy
to point to the sacrificial death of Christ. His death
fulfils every description of purpose. His death fulfils
every description of time. His death fulfils every
description of results. His death makes the ancient
symbols of atonement to become useless thereafter
and to cease. His death becomes the substitution
of a better sacrifice, as seen in the book of Hebrews.
His death precipitates the desolations that must
continue till his people, who rejected him as their
Messiah Prince and thereby made him to "have
nothing," shall be brought to know that he is their
only atonement for sin.

XXVII
Resurrection

Daniel, in 12:2-3, brings the outstanding Old
Testament word concerning the resurrection. He
builds upon such teachings as those found in Job
19:25-27; Psalm 18:10; 17:15; Isaiah 25:8; 26:19;
66:24; Ezekiel 37:1-14. The following points are
made unmistakably clear:

(1) Resurrection from the dead. 12:2a.
(2) Resurrection of the just and the unjust 12:2b
(3) Resurrection unto shining glory for those who are evangelists of the righteousness offered by Messiah. (Cf. righteousness in 12:3 and 9:24.)

Chronological Chart for Study of Daniel and Ezra-Nehemiah

Approximate Dates	Jewish Prophets and Other Leaders	Kings of Babylon and Persia	Contemporary Events in other nations
561 B.C.	Daniel in Babylon	Nebuchadnezzar dies	
561-559		Evil-Merodach	
559-556			
555-538		Nabonidus (Belshazzar regent)	
538-529		Cyrus (Darius the Mede ruler of Babylon 2 yrs.)	Cyrus conquers Media and Lydia
535	Zerubbabel leads first return		
534	Rebuilding Temple begun		
529-522		Cambyses	Cambyses driven from Ethiopia, devastates Egypt
521-486	Haggai and Zechariah	Darius I (Hystaspes)	Battle of Marathon
520	Rebuilding Temple renewed		
516	Temple dedicated		
486-465	Esther and Mordecai save Jews abroad	Xerxes I	Battles of Thermopylae and Salamis
465-425	Ezra leads second return	Artaxerxes I (Longimanus)	Herodotus lives in Greece
458	Nehemiah's first coming		
445	Malachi		
432	Nehemiah comes again		
424		Xerxes II	
424-404		Darius II (Nothus)	
404-359		Artaxerxes II (Mnemon)	
359-336		Artaxerxes III (Ochus)	Alexander conquers Persia
336-330		Darius III (Codomannus)	Death of Alexander
323			
167	Maccabean revolt		
44			Julius Ceasar dies
4	Birth of Jesus		

INTRODUCTION TO EZRA-NEHEMIAH

Parallel Reading

Wilson, R. Dick, "Ezra-Nehemiah," in *ISBE*.

Batten, L. W., "The Books of Ezra and Nehemiah," in *HDB*.

Driver, S. R., *LOT*, chap. XII, sec. 2.

Name, Authorship, and Date

The names of Ezra and Nehemiah have naturally been linked with the books bearing their names because they are the outstanding characters in them. It is also natural to link them together because they treat, for the most part, the same period in Israel's history with the same purpose and method.

Portions of each ascribe themselves to Ezra and Nehemiah by use of the first person. Some think that Ezra and Nehemiah wrote the other portions as well. Some are inclined to favor Ezra as the man that put them in final form. Many, while uncertain as to who he was, think that the final editor was also author of Chronicles.

No exact date can be fixed, but the circumstances point to a time before 400 B.C.

Method and Purpose

These books present a collection of genealogical lists, official papers, letters, memoirs, and chronicles drawn from many sources. The purpose in the whole arrangement is to give evidence that God fulfilled his promise to restore a remnant of his people to their inheritance. (Cf. Ezra 6:14.) They

[272]

do not attempt a history of the period as a whole but stick to the one object of proving JHWH's faithfulness.

OUTLINE

I

Restoration of the Temple. Ezra 1:1 to 6:22

II

Restoration of Judah and Jerusalem.
..................Ezra 7:1 to Nehemiah 13:31

5. Rebuilding of the wall and settlement of the people ....2:9 to 7:73
6. Renewal of the covenant led by Ezra 8:1 to 10:39
    (1) Teaching of the law 8:1-18
    (2) Writing and sealing of a sure covenant 9:1-38
    (3) List of those who sealed this covenant 10:1-39
7. Dedication of Jerusalem by Nehemiah ....11:1 to 13:31
    (1) Selection and blessing of dwellers in Jerusalem ....11:1 to 12:26
    (2) Purification of the priests, the Levites, the people, the gates, and the wall 12:27-30
    (3) Service of dedication 12:31-43
Con. Miscellaneous applications of the dedication: appointment of leaders in the service of the Temple, purging of foreign men from the assembly, bringing in of tithes, keeping of the sabbath, and prohibition of marriages with foreign women ....12:44 to 13:31

INTRODUCTION TO ESTHER

Parallel Reading

Urquhart, John, "Book of Esther," in *ISBE*.
McClymont, J. A., "Book of Esther," in *HDB*.
Driver, S. R., *LOT*, chap. X, sec. 5.

Name, Authorship, and Date

The name is taken from the leading character. Nothing at all is known as to authorship. The thought of Mordecai as the author seems to be excluded by a reference in 10:2-3 to the "full account" of his greatness as "written in the book of the chronicles of the kings of Media and Persia." That seems to take for granted that his life was finished. The same verses make the date after the death of king Ahasuerus, or Xerxes I, as archaeology has shown him to be, which occurred in 465 B.C. Certainly the book reflects the Persian Empire as still strong and glorious, and it is natural to place it before 400 B.C.

Method and Purpose

The book is a dramatic story of God's providential protection of those who fear him. As Ezra-Nehemiah shows God's care of the returning Jewish remnant, so Esther shows his care for the remnant left in exile (Cf. 4:14). An odd fact about the story is that it never mentions God. However, strenuous criticism among Jews and Gentiles has failed to prove any lack of recognition or fear of God. The drama of life is made to reflect conviction of his presence and power. It could be that those Jews in exile tried to reveal the grounds for this conviction to their Gentile associates and themselves without beginning with assumptions as to God's existence, which the use of any name would make, or as to his favor of Israel, such as the use of JHWH would make. 6:13 gives an instance of the spread of such conviction among the Gentiles.

OUTLINE

I
Vashti deposed as queen of Persia..........1:1-22

II
Esther crowned as the new queen..........2:1-18

III
Mordecai saves the life of the king........2:19-23

IV
Haman hates Mordecai for refusal to bow
  down to him 3:1-6

V
Haman chooses by lot a time to kill all Jews 3:7-15

VI
Mordecai and Esther plan to save the Jews 4:1-17

VII
Haman is provoked to build a gallows for
  Mordecai 5:1-14

VIII
King orders Haman to award royal honors
  to Mordecai 6:1-14

INTRODUCTION TO HAGGAI

Parallel Reading

Robinson, George L., "Haggai," in *ISBE*.
Cooke, G. A., "Haggai," in *HDB*.
Driver, S. R., *LOT*, chap. VI, sec. 10.
Kirkpatrick, A. F., *Doctrine of the Prophets,* pp. 413-423f.

Name, Authorship, and Date

The name of the book is that of the prophet. (Cf. 1:1.) It means Festal or Festival of JHWH, but has no evident connection with the message. The prophet doubtless wrote his own messages. All of them were delivered, according to 1:1; 2:1,10,20, in the second year of Darius (Hystaspes), which was 520 B.C. Ezra 5:1 tells us that he and Zechariah worked together to inspire the returned Jews to continue work on the Temple. Zechariah 1:1 tells us that Zechariah began about two months after Haggai. Some think that 2:3 indicates Haggai himself had seen the former Temple. In that case, his life had spanned the captivity and he was old when he began to prophesy. The fact that he prophesies for a few months only, then is heard from no more, accords with this supposition.

Method and Purpose

The purpose of the whole message is to encourage rebuilding of the Temple. Its plan is simple. Four divisions are marked by the four references to dates.

OUTLINE

Rebuilding the Temple

I
Time: 1:1-15

1. It is wrong to say, It is not the time,
   when the people dwell in ceiled houses....1:1-6
2. JHWH punishes the people for delay....1:7-11
   (Zerubbabel and Joshua lead a new
   effort) 1:12-15

II
Glory: 2:1-9

The glory will exceed the glory of the former house 2:1-9

III
Material Benefits: 2:10-19

JHWH will reward the building with prosperity 2:10-19

IV

Establishment of the Rule of Zerubbabel...2:20-23
The political ruler will become a means of
establishing messianic control of the
nations 2:20-23

THEOLOGICAL STUDIES

XXVIII

Value of a House of Worship

While the Temple of Solomon was still standing,
but the people were accepting its ceremonies as substitutes for sincere and spiritual worship, the prophets preached that the Temple was not essential.

When there is no temple and the people tend to forget its worth, the emphasis of the prophets swings to the other side. Haggai gives us outstanding lessons concerning the value of a house of worship in the following ways:

(1) The personal value. In 1:3, Haggai describes the selfish ease which corrupts people's lives when they dwell in good homes and let the house of the Lord lie waste. The cure is zeal on behalf of that house of worship. In 1:13 the reward of such zeal is Jehovah's assurance, "I am with you." Nothing has a higher personal value than that assurance, and loyalty to the worship of God's house is a chief means by which God gives it.

(2) The religious value. In 2:9, Haggai predicts a greater glory for the new Temple than for the old. Fulfilment does not necessarily come through a more magnificent building. The means whereby this glory is to be brought to the new Temple are described in 2:6-7, and they are messianic. Even so, every house of true worship, humble or magnificent, makes its worshipers participants in the glory of Messiah's kingdom. By their maintenance of religious services they furnish a means for the spread of that glory.

(3) The material value. In 2:11-13, Haggai draws an illustration from the priestly ritual to indicate that evil spreads more rapidly than good. In 2:14-17, he goes on to apply this to Israel's life. He shows that neglect of worship as God willed it was polluting the people's whole life, making the

half-hearted efforts they had made unacceptable to God, and making it necessary for him to withhold material benefits.

(4) The political value. In 2:23, Haggai says that JHWH will make Zerubbabel his signet, or ring with a seal for authorization of official documents. This indicates that he will use Zerubbabel, the political ruler, as another ordained means of establishing the rule of Messiah. (Cf. 2:21-22.) The time is "in that day," the time of the fulfilment of the preceding promises about the Temple. Thus God's purpose for political rule is to be fulfilled as it helps fulfil his purpose for worship. Thus are the interests of true worship and a godly state bound together. Their functions are separate but the destinies of both are to be fulfilled by establishment of the kingdom of God.

INTRODUCTION TO ZECHARIAH

Parallel Reading

Robinson, George L., "Book of Zechariah," in *ISBE*

Nowack, W., "Book of Zechariah," in *HDB*.
Driver, S. R., *LOT*, chap. VI, sec. 11.
Kirkpatrick, A. F., *Doctrine of the Prophets,* pp. 424-478.

Name, Authorship, and Date

1:1 and 7:1 show that the name of the book is that of the author of chapters 1-8. Only two other headings appear in the book. They are in 9:1 and 12:1, and they do not name date or author. 1:1 does show that the visions of chapters 1-6 came in the second year of Darius (Hystaspes), which was 520 B.C. 7:1 puts the message of chapters 7-8 in 518 B.C.

Opinions vary greatly concerning the authorship and date of chapters 9-14. There are no indications as to date or author except the fact that they are attached to the writings of Zechariah. Some put them before the captivity, some long after the time of Zechariah, some during the latter years of his life. The messages of these chapters look entirely to the future. They may have grown gradually through many years. These facts could account for the lack of dates. If Zechariah was a young man when the messages of chapters 1-8 were received, the lapse of years would account for other differences. Thus it appears most probable that these chapters are the fruit of Zechariah's mature years.

Method and Purpose

The four main divisions are indicated by the headings already mentioned. The first includes an introductory word followed by eight visions, all of which bring messages of encouragement concerning the building of the Temple. The second answers questions about fasting which arose because the Temple was being rebuilt. While the other two are complicated and offer many difficulties in interpretation, yet it is evident that an interpretation of the future of the house of JHWH runs through them. They begin in 9:8 with a promise of its protection from the nations by JHWH. They close in 14:21 with the saying, "There shall be no more a Canaanite in the house of Jehovah of hosts," meaning that all who worship in it in that day will be truly the people of JHWH. Thus we see that the most obvious purpose of Zechariah was to interpret the meaning of the Temple to the people of JHWH.

On the other hand, there is a less obvious but infinitely more significant purpose running through all these divisions. There is a deeply spiritual interpretation that clothes itself in an apocalyptic style, addresses itself to eschatological problems, and finds their solution in Messiah. The interpretation of Messiah so dominates the entire book that there seems to be full warrant for this claim of George L. Robinson, "No other book is as Messianic."[1] The interpretation of the Temple is simply a stepping-stone to this.

[1] Robinson, George L., "Book of Zechariah," *ISBE*, p. 31-36.

OUTLINE

Introduction: 1:1-6

Restoration depends upon repentance......1:1-6

I
Rebuilding of the Temple: 1:7 to 6:15

1. Vision of a man riding upon a red horse 1:7-17
   It assures the restoration of Jerusalem (Cf. 9:16-17)

2. Vision of four horns and four smiths 1:18-21
   It assures the overthrow of Jerusalem's enemies (Cf. 1:21b)

3. Vision of a man with a measuring line 2:1-13
   It assures the increase of Jerusalem's people (Cf. 2:4,11)

4. Vision of a change of the garments of the High Priest......................3:1-10
   It assures the cleansing of the land by "the Branch" (Cf. 3:4,9)

5. Vision of a candlestick fed from two olive trees 4:1-14
   It assures victory through the Holy Spirit of JHWH and two anointed ones (Cf. 4:6,14)

6. Vision of a flying roll..................5:1-4
   It assures destruction of the wicked (Cf. 5:4)

THEOLOGICAL STUDIES
XXIX

Final Recognition of Messiah by Israel

Zechariah's pictures of Messiah are filled with an atmosphere of mystery. The result is that we are completely mystified at times. Nevertheless, we are confident that the prophetic writers desired that their writings be understood. We know that there were good reasons why their messages were clothed in apocalyptic symbols, but also that the use of symbols called for a key to open the door for the initiated. In this case the key appears to be in 14:9. This verse sees final recognition of the unity of JHWH as a crowning development of that day when the universal kingdom of God is established. When we find in earlier chapters that the author identifies JHWH with the Angel of JHWH and also the angel with the Branch of David, we realize that this final recognition of JHWH as one means final recognition by Israel that Messiah is not merely the divine-Davidic king, but also the high priestly Saviour of Israel, the Angel of JHWH, the glory of Israel, the Holy One of Israel, even JHWH manifested unto men.

Zechariah prepares the way for his prediction of this recognition by skilfully interweaving into his messages about the Temple mysterious intimations that the identity of the many diverse manifestations of Messiah is not generally recognized. Then, in chapters 9-11, he pictures him coming in lowly form as the shepherd of the poor and being rejected by the false shepherds. Then, in chapters 12-14, he sees the final recognition of him as "me [JHWH] whom they have pierced." Thus he leads us to the best Old Testament view of the great final crisis in Israel's history.

Identity of His Many Diverse Manifestations

In the visions of chapters 1-6 it is quite difficult at first to keep in mind who is who. Careful observation, however, gives one the impression that the situation which thus baffles us was calculated to call attention to a series of identifications which lead to a very surprising result.

In 1:8, a man is described as standing "among the myrtle-trees." In 1:9, this man is addressed as "my lord," described further as "the angel that talked with me," and he promises to answer a question concerning the horses seen in the vision. In 1:10, it is "the man . . . among the myrtle-trees" that answers, and, in 1:11, he is called "the angel of Jehovah." Furthermore, in 1:13, "the angel of Jehovah" is called "the angel that talked with me." Thus all descriptions apply to the angel of JHWH.

These same descriptions identify the medium of revelation in all the other visions as the angel of JHWH. (Cf. 1:19; 2:3; 3:1; 4:1; 5:2,5; 6:4.)

In 1:19-21, the angel is addressed, and JHWH answers. In 2:8-11, the work of JHWH is ascribed both to JHWH and to the angel of JHWH. 2:3 shows that the angel of JHWH sends the message of JHWH to the prophet. Thus, in 2:8, "he" refers to JHWH and "me" to the angel. In 2:10, JHWH says, "I will dwell in the midst of thee." So the presence of the angel is the presence of JHWH. In 3:1-10, these teachings are given pointed application as the angel exercises the prerogatives of God in directing that the filthy garments of Joshua, or his iniquity as shown by 3:4, be changed to clean ones, or righteousness.

In 2:8, the angel says that JHWH hath sent him "after glory"; i. e., in pursuit of glory, or to secure glory. In 6:13, the Branch, who is of course the messianic branch of David described in Isaiah 4:2; Jeremiah 23:5; 33:15; Zechariah 3:8; 6:12, is pointed out as the one to "bear the glory." Thus the angel is identified with the Branch. This means that Messiah is to fulfil both the priestly and kingly functions in Israel. This helps us to understand the symbolism of the fifth vision. In 4:14, the two olive branches are interpreted as "the two anointed ones, that stand by the Lord of the whole earth." They are the heads of the religious and the political life of Israel. The spiritual power of JHWH is to be exercised through both. The ordained purpose for both will be fulfilled through Messiah.

When it is said, in 14:9, "in that day shall Jehovah be one, and his name one," recognition by JHWH's people of these identifications is foreseen. All theophanies are appearances of Messiah. JHWH who walked in Eden; the Angel of JHWH who led Abraham, Isaac, Jacob, Moses, Joshua, Samuel, David, and the prophets; the one in the cloud over the Red Sea, Mount Sinai, the Tabernacle, and the

Temple; the prophet like unto Moses; the David
their king of Hosea 3:5; the ruler in Israel to be
born in Bethlehem according to Micah 5:2; the
Holy One of Israel whom Isaiah pictured as a divine-Davidic king, a suffering successful Saviour,
and a glorious glorifying redeemer; Jeremiah's
maker of the new covenant; Ezekiel's reigning
glory; Daniel's son of man and Messiah-prince;
Zechariah's shepherd of the flock of slaughter and
Pierced One; all become one, the good shepherd of
Israel.

Rejection of Him as a Shepherd of the Poor

Coming before this wonderful recognition as one,
Zechariah saw a tragic and terrible period in which
Messiah would appear as a shepherd of the poor
and be rejected. This comes out in chapters 9-11.
It builds upon Isaiah 52:13 to 53:12 and Daniel,
chapter 9.

In 9:1-10, the king is seen coming unto Jerusalem, "just, and having salvation; lowly, and riding
upon an ass, even upon a colt the foal of an ass."
It is obvious that Jesus presented himself as the
fulfilment of this prophecy at the time of the
Triumphal Entry. We need to note especially his
lowly form, for this accounts for the rejection that
follows.

In 11:12-13, the appointed shepherd is despised
by worthless shepherds of Israel, who despise him
and accept thirty pieces of silver as his hire. According to Exodus 21:32, thirty pieces of silver is
the amount of damages to be paid in case a slave

is killed. The passage thus predicts acceptance of this price for his life and is fulfilled in Judas' sale of Jesus for that amount. We need to note especially the consequences. God's side of these consequences is described in 11:10-11 as a breaking of his covenant with these false elements of Israel. This is understood and accepted by the poor of the flock as the will of God. Israel's side of these consequences is seen in 11:15-17 as another deliverance of Israel into the hands of worthless rulers for a period of selfish, cruel, devastating control, destined for woe.

Final Recognition of Him as Me (JHWH)
Whom They Pierced

Finally the picture changes. In chapters 12-14, Zechariah goes beyond all others in viewing the circumstances of the great crisis in the establishment of the kingdom of God, which bring about Israel's long delayed recognition of him.

In 12:10, this recognition is seen as coming in a time of mourning. This may be due partly to the effects of the great world struggle it follows, pictured in 12:1-9. The all-inclusive cause, however, is that this recognition of Messiah is recognition of "me [JHWH] whom they have pierced." Unless the foregoing identifications have been faithfully followed, the use of me in this clause and the switch to him in the parallel clauses that follow are apt to be upsetting. However, they stand in the accepted Hebrew text as a bold challenge to us to accept Zechariah's teaching that rejection of the lowly Messiah is rejection of JHWH and acceptance of Messiah's redemption will be acceptance of the sovereignty of JHWH. Such recognition by Israel will of course be a time of mourning for the sin that despised and crucified him at his first coming.

In 13:1 this recognition is described as the opening of "a fountain . . . to the house of David and to the inhabitants of Jerusalem, for sin and for uncleanness." Thus the mourning that precedes is repentant mourning, and the rule that succeeds is a spiritual rule.

In 13:8-9, this recognition is given by a remnant of a remnant of Israel. Two-thirds of the remnant that returned to the land is seen as destroyed, and the remaining third is brought into the fire, there, in the land, so as to bring about mutual recognition between JHWH and Israel.

Conclusion

Thus 14:9 can say, "Jehovah shall be king over all the earth." The oneness of this JHWH who will be king and the JHWH whom man cannot see is not a oneness of person, but of spirit, work, and authority. It is a unity like that ideal spiritual unity described in Genesis 2:24 as God's will for husband and wife. The same word is used in both cases. Thus, when Moses says in Deuteronomy 6:4, "Jehovah our God is one Jehovah," he describes the absence of any moral conflict or division in the rule of the Godhead. Thus Jesus can say, "All authority hath been given unto me in heaven and on earth" (Matt. 28:18).

INTRODUCTION TO MALACHI

Parallel Reading

Robinson, George L., "Malachi," in *ISBE*.
Welch, A. C., "Malachi," in *HDB*.
Driver, S. R., *LOT*, chap. VI, sec. 12.
Kirkpatrick, A. F., *Doctrine of the Prophets*,
    chap. XVII.

Name, Authorship, and Date

The name Malachi, which appears in 1:1 of our
text, means my messenger. The original word corresponds exactly to "my messenger" in 3:1. For
this reason some think the word in 1:1 was not intended to be a proper name. The LXX translated
it "my messenger." However, the fact that all other
writing prophets are named and the fact that this
word appears where the name of the author usually
appears warrants us in accepting it as the name of
the prophet.

Apart from this book we know nothing about
Malachi. It tells us very little. It does reflect con-
ditions which parallel those described by Ezra and
Nehemiah, and it fits best the situation existing after
Nehemiah's first visit and before his return from
Persia. Thus a date shortly before 432 B.C. is
chosen.

Method and Purpose

Malachi's style is simple, prosaic, and dialectic.
After a teaching fashion, often employing questions
and answers, he tackles the great problems in Israel's life. Step by step he shows how the love of

[292]

JHWH will prove his choice of Israel. He sees a time during which JHWH's curse will rest upon the nation because of refusal to honor him, while his name is great among the Gentiles, but also a time beyond in which Israel is healed by the coming of the Lord, the messenger of the covenant, the Sun of righteousness. Thus JHWH's love proves his election of Jacob rather than Esau.

OUTLINE
(Title: 1:1)

THEOLOGICAL STUDIES
XXX
Material Prosperity for God's People

The promise of Malachi 3:10 that material blessings will result from bringing tithes and offerings to the support of the Lord's work is the high point of much Old Testament teaching concerning material blessings for the people of God. It is very important, yet easily abused by misunderstanding. The following facts about it need to be made plain:

1. The promise is made to Israel as a nation. When the nation as a whole orders its economy so as to foster worship of JHWH, teaching of his law, faithful leadership, and righteous living by all, material blessings are seen as an inevitable consequence. This may result in the case of individuals or small groups. Over the period of a lifetime it generally does so. However, when those surrounding a righteous man are unscrupulous, covetous, and predatory, "he that departeth from evil maketh himself a prey" (Isa. 59:15).

2. The promise makes material blessings a fruitage of righteousness. It is not the mere bringing of tithes and offerings but the bringing of them as a part of a righteous life that produces these results. They are not the "rake off" of wickedness, currying favor by a division of spoils. They are the fruit of such industry, order, honesty, frugality, wise use of gain, and the like as develops in the living of those who love God.

3. The promise is applicable to any people. Because it is an application of spiritual principles, this

promise is applicable to all peoples who fear the
Lord. The nature of the fulfilment will differ, but
the promise will fit all.

XXXI

Forerunner of Messiah

In 3:1-3, Malachi pictures Messiah as the Angel
of the Covenant, coming to purge Israel. In 4:2, he
pictures him as the Sun of righteousness with healing in his beams. The last word in this description
means in general either wings or beams, but the
connection with the sun here makes beams prefer-
able. Both these descriptions parallel previous messianic teaching.

In 4:4-6, Malachi adds a new messianic element.
He predicts a forerunner for the Messiah. Jesus, in
Matthew 11:14, pointed to the fulfilment of this in
John the Baptist.